Student Almanac of Hispanic American History

Volume 1: From European Contact

to the U.S.-Mexican War,

1492–1848

Student Almanac of Hispanic American History

Volume 1: From European Contact to the U.S.-Mexican War, 1492–1848

GREENWOOD PRESS

Westport, Connecticut • London

Library of Congress Cataloging-in-Publication Data
Student almanac of Hispanic American history / by Media Projects, Inc.
    p. cm
    Includes bibliographical references and indexes.
  Contents: v. 1. From European contact to the U.S.-Mexican War, 1492–1848—v. 2. From
the California Gold Rush to today, 1849–present.
ISBN 0–313–32605–3 (set : alk. paper)—ISBN 0–313–32606–1 (v. 1 : alk. paper)—
ISBN 0–313–32607–X (v. 2 : alk. paper)
  1. Hispanic Americans—History—Miscellanea—Juvenile literature. 2. Hispanic
Americans—History—Sources—Juvenile literature. 3. Almanacs, American—Juvenile
literature. [1. Hispanic Americans—History—Miscellanea. 2. Hispanic
Americans—History—Sources.] I. Media Projects Incorporated.
E184.S75S78 2004
973'.0468—dc21   2003044824

British Library Cataloguing in Publication Data is available.

Library of Congress Catalog Card Number: 2003044824
ISBN: 0–313–32605–3 (set)
       0–313–32606–1 (Vol. 1)
       0–313–32607–X (Vol. 2)

First published in 2004

Greenwood Press, 88 Post Road West, Westport, CT 06881
An imprint of Greenwood Publishing Group, Inc.
www.greenwood.com

Printed in the United States of America

The paper used in this book complies with the
Permanent Paper Standard issued by the National
Information Standards Organization (Z39.48–1984).

10 9 8 7 6 5 4 3 2 1

A Media Projects, Inc. Production

Editor: Carter Smith
Production Editor and Cartographer: Jim Burmester
Design: Amy Henderson
Contributing Writers: Wordwise, Inc.
Copyediting: Emerald Editorial Services, Inc.
Indexer: Jim Burmester

CONTENTS

Volume 1: From European Contact to the U.S.-Mexican War, 1492–1848

From European Contact to the U.S.-Mexican War

1492–1848

"They came in battle array, as conquerors, and the dust rose in whirlwinds on the roads [and] their spears glinted in the sun."

—An Aztec describing the Spanish arriving in the Valley of Mexico

In 1492, **Christopher Columbus** (see p. 52), an Italian-born explorer, who was sailing ships given to him by **King Ferdinand and Queen Isabella** (see p. 25) of **Spain** (see p. 39), sighted what would become the Bahamas on October 12.

Columbus and his men were not the first Europeans to reach the Americas. The Viking Leif Ericsson had reached Newfoundland in 1000. But Columbus was the first to establish settlements in what Europeans called the New World. Columbus and the Spaniards who followed him had come to stay.

Most of *Student Almanac of Hispanic American History, Volume 1* concerns the roughly 350 years that followed Columbus's arrival. However, to understand Hispanic American history, one must recognize that the Spanish side of Hispanic American history is only part of the story. Even the term "Hispanic American" doesn't tell the whole story. Unlike other minority groups in the United States, such as African Americans, the term "Hispanic Americans" has nothing to do with race. Hispanic Americans can be Caucasian, African, or Native American. (There are even Hispanics of Asian ancestry.) Usually, they are a mixture of some or all of the above. What unites them as Hispanic Americans is the Spanish language they speak.

THE DIVERSE HISPANIC HERITAGE

Chapter One of *Student Almanac of Hispanic American History* outlines histories of the three main ethnic groups that make up the Hispanic American heritage. In reading about ancient Spanish history, students will find that Spain has had a long history of diversity. The people of Spain are a mixture of many groups, including **Iberians** (see p. 27), **Phoenicians** (see p. 34), **Celts** (see p. 23), Romans, **Vandals** (see p. 40), **Visigoths** (see p. 41), and **Moors** (see p. 31).

When Columbus reached what he first thought was Asia, he did not find the land unoccupied. Instead, he and the Spaniards who followed him would find the land populated with hundreds of different Native American civilizations. Many of these civilizations, such as the **Aztec** (see p. 20), **Maya** (see p. 29), and **Inca** (see p. 27), were very advanced, as well as powerful and wealthy. Although contact with the Spanish and other Europeans often brought death from war and disease to the Native American peoples, Spaniards and Native Americans also bore children together. In time, a **mestizo** (see p. 62), or mixed race of part Spaniard, part Native American would become the most common racial group among Hispanic Americans.

Finally, Chapter One of *Student Almanac of Hispanic American History* discusses the influence of Africans on Hispanic America. Readers may be surprised to learn that while about half a million enslaved Africans were seized from West Africa and brought directly to the British colonies of North America during colonial times, three times that many were brought to Spanish colonies in Central America and the Caribbean. The rich cultures of West Africa would become another powerful influence on Hispanic American culture.

EMPIRE IN THE AMERICAS

In Chapter Two of *Student Almanac of Hispanic American History*, readers will learn about how Spain created a vast empire in the Americas that stretched throughout much of the Caribbean, as well as South, Central, and North America. This chapter covers the adventures of famous **conquistadors** (see p. 54) like **Hernán Cortés** (see p. 55), who destroyed the Aztec Empire of Central Mexico and **Juan Pizzaro** (see p. 68), who did the same to the Inca Empire of Peru. Students will also learn about explorers like **Coronado** (see p. 54), **De Soto** (see p. 56), **Balboa** (see p. 51), **Ponce de León** (see p. 69), and others, who explored what is now the United States as far north as Virginia on the Atlantic and the state of Washington on the Pacific.

They may also be surprised to discover that the oldest European settlements in the United States are not the English settlements at Jamestown in Virginia or Plymouth in Massachusetts, but the Spanish settlements in St. Augustine, **Florida** (see p. 58), and Santa Fe, **New Mexico** (see p. 66).

From their capital in Mexico City, the Spanish controlled a large empire known as New Spain. Over the course of about three hundred years, Spain held more land in the Americas than any other European power. By the mid-1600s however, other European countries, especially England and France, began to challenge them for control. By the time of the **American Revolution** (see p. 79) in 1776, Spain's power in the Americas had weakened. However, students will learn how Spain helped the American patriots during the American Revolution in order to win back land lost to the British.

In Chapter Two, readers will also discover that Spain's Catholic **missions** (see p. 64) of **California** (see p. 104), built between the 1770s and 1820s, were not only built for religious reasons. The missions also helped Spain guard against other nations settling lands in Spain's **Far North** (see p. 106), as the northern frontier of New Spain was known.

INDEPENDENCE FROM SPAIN

Despite efforts to protect their power in North America, by the early nineteenth century, Spain's New World empire was ready to collapse. However, the reason was not because of challenges from other Europeans. Instead, it was from independence movements that swept through most of Spain's colonies. During the early nineteenth century, one former Spanish colony after another gained independence from Spain. Readers will learn about Simon Bolivar, who liberated much of South America. They will also learn about Father Miguel Hidalgo, a Mexican priest who started a revolution that would win Mexico its independence (see **Mexican War of Independence** p. 84).

THE UNITED STATES AND "MANIFEST DESTINY"

After winning independence from Spain, Mexico quickly faced a new challenge—this time from the United States. In Chapter Four, readers will learn how American settlers in **Texas** (see p. 91), joined by some Tejanos (Hispanic Texans), challenged the authority of the Mexican government. This conflict would turn into a drive for war for independence. Texans like **Sam Houston** (see p. 107) and **Stephen Austin** (see p. 102) would go down in history, as would the famous **Battle of the Alamo** (see p. 99).

A few years after winning independence from Mexico, the new Republic of Texas, also called the **Lone Star Republic** (see p. 109) entered the United States as a new state. However, the United States had its sights on more than Texas. Ever since 1803, when the United States purchased the **Louisiana Territory** (see p. 61) from France, American explorers, trappers, and adventurers had moved westward—often into Mexican territory. In 1846, the United States launched a war on Mexico (see **U.S.-Mexican war** p. 124). Within two years, American troops had captured Mexico City, and the United States had forced Mexico to give up its vast lands in the Far North.

HOW TO USE THIS BOOK

Each chapter in *Student Almanac of Hispanic American History* is divided into two parts. The first part is a short essay that gives a summary of the major events in that time in Hispanic American history. The second part is an A–Z section that describes many important people, events, and terms that have to do with the time period.

To help readers find related ideas more easily, many terms are cross-indexed. Within both the essay and A–Z section of each chapter, some words appear in **bold letters**, followed by a page number. That means the term is also a separate A–Z entry in the book which should be read for more information. In each chapter's timeline, words appearing as entries in that chapter's A–Z section are also highlighted. Other unfamiliar words are printed in ***bold italics***. Short definitions of these words can be found in a glossary that begins on page 129. Finally, words that may be hard to pronounce are followed by a pronunciation key.

CHAPTER ONE

The Roots of Hispanic America

Spain, Africa, and Native America, Prehistory–1491

"At no time in history has there been such a significant degree of culture contact between peoples of completely distinct traditions."

—George Foster, 1960

What does the term *Hispanic* (*his-PAN-ik*) mean? Where are Hispanic people from? How did they develop their culture and language? *Hispanic* describes a very large group of people from many different cultures and races. These people share one important cultural feature—their Spanish language. The Hispanic people have a history that spans thousands of years and many continents. The peoples of Europe, Africa, and North and South America have all contributed to the Hispanic culture.

The story of the Hispanic people begins on the peninsula where modern **Spain** (see p. 39) and **Portugal** (see p. 35) are located. Prehistoric paintings found in Spain show that humans had already been living in that region for more than six thousand years when a new group of people arrived. Around 3000 B.C.E. the **Iberians** (*eye-BEER-ee-ins*) (see p. 27) of North Africa crossed the Strait of **Gibraltar** (*jib-RAWL-ter*) (see p. 26) to the peninsula. The Iberian people were farmers and warriors. They built fortified towns and established trade among their own tribes and with people from other lands. The peninsula became known as the **Iberian Peninsula** (see p. 27).

By 1200 B.C.E., the **Phoenicians** (*fuh-NEE-shuns*) (see p. 34) had discovered the natural ports along the peninsula's coast. The Phoenicians were

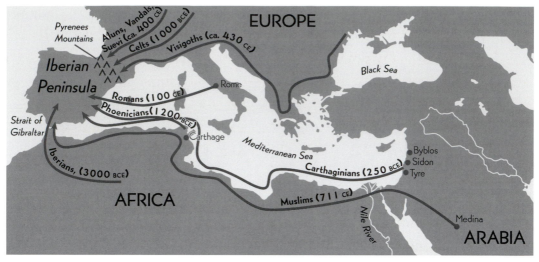

The Iberian Peninsula, where modern-day Spain and Portugal are located, has been the meeting place of people from many civilizations. Because of this, Spanish culture has been a mix of many different influences. In the Americas, the Spanish would later blend even more by coming into contact with Native American and African peoples.

famous sailors and merchants who traveled the seas of the known world. They traded with the Iberians and also built towns of their own on the peninsula. During their trading trips to other lands, Phoenicians let the rest of the world know about the Iberians. Greeks soon came to the Iberian Peninsula to trade, as did some early Romans.

The first major invasion of the Iberian Peninsula came from the north. Around 1000 B.C.E., a group of people called **Celts** (*KELTS*) (see p. 23) came over the Pyrenees (*PEER-uh-nees*) Mountains. The Celts had traveled from

Timeline

3000 B.C.E.

North African peoples cross the Strait of **Gibraltar** into the **Iberian Peninsula**. They became the **Iberians**.

1200 B.C.E.

The **Phoenicians** arrive on the Iberian Peninsula. They establish trade with the Iberian peoples.

Olmec civilization in **Mesoamerica** flourishes.

the northern and eastern parts of the European continent. Like the original Iberians, the Celts were farmers and warriors. The arrival of the Celts signaled the first of many times when the people living on the Iberian Peninsula would blend their culture with another. Over the course of more than seven hundred years, the Celts intermarried with the Iberians. In time, the two groups became one group. They were called the **Celtiberians** (*KELT-uh-BEER-ee-uns*) (see p. 21). The Celtiberians developed a new culture that drew from both their Iberian and Celtic ancestors.

The next major invasion occurred around 250 B.C.E. The Carthaginians (*kar-thuh-JIN-ee-ins*) came from a very powerful Phoenician city in North Africa. They conquered the Iberian Peninsula. Like the Celts, the Carthaginians brought their own customs and beliefs. These became folded into the traditions of the Celtiberians.

Within a hundred years, the Romans had replaced the Carthaginians as the new rulers. **Rome** (see p. 38) was the most powerful nation in the world of its day. Romans had an important and lasting influence on the people of the Iberian Peninsula. They built roads and established a system of law. Most important, the Romans brought the language that is the basis of modern-day Spanish. This helped to unify the empire. It also opened it to greater opportunities for trade. Rome called this conquered land Hispania (*HIS-pan-ya*), which became the basis for the English name, Spain.

Spain was under Roman rule for over six hundred years. During that

1000 B.C.E.	**250 B.C.E.**	**201 B.C.E.**	**100 C.E.**
Celts cross the Pyrenees into the **Iberian Peninsula**. They establish colonies and begin to blend their culture with the **Iberians**.	Carthaginians cross the Strait of **Gibraltar** to the **Iberian Peninsula**. They defeat the **Celtiberians**.	**Rome** defeats the Carthaginians in **Spain**. Four hundred years of Roman rule begins.	The Christian religion is introduced into **Spain**. The **Akimel O'odham**, or **Pima**, peoples establish their nation in southwest Arizona.

time, wars were fought there and territory was both gained and lost. Many Roman soldiers retired to Spain when their terms of service were over. They often married women of Celtiberian and Carthaginian heritage, and their descendents blended all three cultures.

In the first century of the common era, the Christian religion was introduced into Spain. Many peoples of the Iberian Peninsula practiced the new religion. They mixed into the religion their own local *pagan* customs and traditions. By the fourth century C.E., Christianity was practiced throughout Spain. It became a very important part of the area's culture. Christianity had a critical influence on the actions of kings, queens, explorers, and priests over the coming centuries. It was one of the reasons that the people of Spain became the conquerors instead of the conquered in the fifteenth century.

Christianity was not the only religion to enter the region at this time. Judaism (*JU-dee-is-um*) also established itself in Spain. Jews had been expelled from their homeland in eastern Europe. They found Spain to be a safe haven. Jewish philosophers and physicians brought their ancient knowledge and culture with them. This added yet another unique layer to the Hispanic tradition.

By 409 C.E., Rome was weakening. It no longer was the world power it had been. Other nations looked to Spain as a rich jewel they would like to own. They took advantage of Rome's weakness and invaded the Iberian Peninsula. These new invaders were Germanic peoples from the north. The

200

Moche peoples build a civilization in Peru.

300

Maya peoples begin a period of great advances in **Mesoamerica**.

The **Chavin** peoples of Peru develop the culture that will influence all other Andean nations that follow.

409

Germanic peoples invade **Spain**. These nations include the Alans, **Vandals**, and Suevi. Roman era ends in **Spain**.

412

Visigoths enter **Spain** and drive out the other Germanic nations. This begins 300 years of Visigothic rule in **Spain**.

Alans (*AL-uns*), **Vandals** (*VAN-duls*) (see p. 40), and Suevi (*SWAY-vi*) crossed the Pyrenees just as the Celts had done hundreds of years before. Also like the Celts, they came to stay. They were followed by an even more powerful Germanic tribe called the **Visigoths** (*VIZ-ih-goths*) (see p. 41). For three hundred years, the Visigoths ruled much like the Romans did, with similar laws and customs. They also introduced their own northern Germanic customs.

By then, the people of the Iberian Peninsula were a nation whose inhabitants carried the blood of North Africans, eastern Europeans, Romans, and Germanic tribes. They were a Christian nation with a religion that also blended many traditions. The Hispanic character was being formed, year after year. The shaping of that character was not yet complete. The next wave of invaders would bring sweeping change once again.

In the seventh century, a new religion had begun in Arabia. The religion was called Islam (*iz-LAHM*) and its followers were Muslims (*MUZ-lims*). As the Muslims grew in number, their armies rolled over the entire Arabian peninsula. Many powerful empires fell. The armies turned to North Africa and soon captured all the territory from Egypt to Tripoli. Most of the people in the conquered territories became Muslim. In North Africa, a tribe of *nomads* called Berbers (*BER-bers*) accepted Islam. The Berbers were also known as the **Moors** (see p. 31). In 711 C.E., the Moors decided to cross the Strait of Gibraltar to Spain.

500	**711–718**	**711–718**	**722**
The kingdom of Ghana becomes the most powerful nation in **West Africa**. Ghana gains control of the trade routes through the Sahara.	**Moors** cross the Strait of **Gibraltar** to **Spain**. They capture **Cordoba**, Toledo, and Seville. Most of the **Iberian Peninsula** comes under Moorish rule.	**Natchez** civilization begins in the southeastern area of North America. **Pueblo** nation enters a time of growth in the southwestern area of North America.	**Reconquista** begins. At the Battle of Covadonga, the Visigothic leader, Pelayo, stops the advance of the **Moors** into **Spain**. The **Reconquista** continues for the next 800 years.

Like the Romans before them, the Moors from North Africa brought a great deal of change to the people of Spain. These new invaders ruled most of the Iberian Peninsula for the next seven hundred years. The influence of the Moors on Hispanic culture was very important. From the eighth through the twelfth centuries C.E., most of Europe was experiencing a time of ignorance and superstition called the Dark Ages. For the people of Spain, however, it was a time of learning. Under Moorish rule, Spain led the world in science, architecture, literature, and art.

Almost from the time the Moors first arrived, the Christian kings they defeated tried to drive them out. The Christian kings called this effort the **Reconquista** (*ray-con-KEES-tuh*) (see p. 37), the "reconquering." Although it took hundreds of years, the Christian kings eventually succeeded. In the fifteenth century C.E., **Ferdinand II of Aragon and Isabella I of Castile** (see p. 25) united their kingdoms and drove out the last of the Moorish rulers. This united Spain under Christian rule. Once unified, the kingdoms that would become Spain and Portugal began their own era of invasion. They led the world in exploring and blending their own culture with other cultures around the world. While Spain was going through thousands of years of growth, these cultures also grew.

From the fifth to the twelfth century C.E., the kingdom of Ghana (*GAH-nuh*) ruled **West Africa** (see p. 41) south of the Sahara Desert. It established important trade in enslaved peoples and gold with cities in North

929	**1025**	**1094**	**1139**
Moorish **Spain** begins an age of great advances in the sciences, literature, and medicine.	The **Navajo** people move into the southwest area of North America.	**El Cid** captures the Moorish city of Valencia.	King Alfonso Henriques declares **Portugal**'s independence from **Spain**.

Africa. In the thirteenth century, the kingdom of Benin (*ben-EEN*) became more powerful than Ghana. The people of Benin were famous for beautiful works of art in bronze. By the middle of the fifteenth century C.E. Spanish and Portuguese merchants had begun trade with several West African nations. Within two hundred years, that trade included enslaved people for the new lands soon to be discovered on the other side of the world. These lands were North and South America.

In 1200 B.C.E., ancient civilizations had long existed in the Americas. In eastern Mexico, the **Olmec** (*OHL-mek*) (see p. 33) people were building large pyramid temples. By 300 C.E., the **Maya** (*MY-UH*) (see p. 29) had made great achievements in mathematics and writing. A calendar they created is still in use in some parts of Mexico today. In the fourteenth century C.E., the **Aztec** (*AZ-TEK*) (see p. 20) built an empire that included a city of 250,000 people. In South America, the **Inca** (*IN-cuh*) (see p. 27) built strong roads to connect all of their important cities. Despite all these civilizations' accomplishments, they did not know about the existence of the European continent and its peoples.

In the vast lands of North America, hundreds of different Native American nations had established their own histories. The **Pueblo** (*PWEB-loh*) (see p. 36) people in the southwestern part of the continent had built cliff dwellings that could house hundreds of people. They created beautiful works of art in pottery and fabrics. The **Akimel O'odham** (*ah-KEE-mel OH-uhd-uhm*)

1200	1236	1325	1419
The **Inca** settle in the valley of Cuzco in Peru.	The Christian armies recapture **Cordoba** from the **Moors**.	The **Aztec** start to build their capital city of Tenochtitlán.	Portuguese ships begin to explore the western coast of Africa.

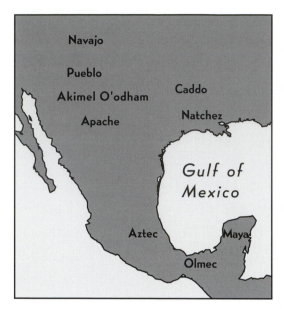

Native American peoples of what are now Latin America and the Southwest United States mixed with Spanish settlers and Africans to create a new, mixed culture. The locations of several examples of Native American nations are given on this map.

(see p. 19) had an advanced system of *irrigation* to bring water to their fields.

Within a very short period of time, the peoples of North and South America would come into contact with a new race of people. These people would come from Spain, a land with its own history of blended cultures and traditions. The newcomers would change the lives of the people in the Americas. Native Americans would also change the lives of the invaders from Spain. Together, they would create yet another culture, filled with new traditions. That culture would be what is called today the Hispanic American culture.

1450

Prince Henry of **Portugal** establishes a school to teach navigation, astronomy, and mapmaking.

The **Arawak** nation is flourishing in the Caribbean.

1469

Ferdinand II of Aragon and Isabella I of Castile marry. This unites two of the largest Spanish kingdoms into one.

1478

The **Spanish Inquisition** begins.

1491

Christian armies drive the **Moors** out of Granada. This completes the **Reconquista**.

A-Z of Key People, Places, and Terms

Akimel O'odham (ah-KEE-mel OH-uhd-uhm) (Pima)

Southwestern Native American nation that was one of the first to come in contact with Spanish explorers in the sixteenth century. The Akimel O'odham, whom the Spanish called the Pima, lived along the Salt and Gila (*HEE-luh*) Rivers in what is now southwest Arizona. Their culture thrived from about 100 B.C.E. to 1500 C.E. The Pima were very successful farmers. They developed an *irrigation* system to help bring water from the river to their fields of corn, beans, squash, and cotton. The men also hunted small game and fished. The women gathered wild plants such as cactus fruits for food. They also wove baskets and made pottery. The men wove cotton for clothing. Pima houses were about seven feet high and shaped like a dome. They were thatched with brush and covered with clay.

Like many Native American nations, the Pima had an elected chief who led councils. The chief and council made decisions about projects that involved all the people in the village. They also worked on ways to defend the people from enemies. The Apache were a particular problem because they often raided the Pima settlements. The location of the Pima settlements also made it easier for them to trade with other nations. The Pima were one of the Native American nations with whom the **Mesoamerican** (*MEZ-oh-uh-mair-ih-can*) (see p. 29) people traded.

Arawak

Caribbean native nation. The Arawak (*AIR-uh-wak*) were descended from peoples living in the central Amazon region of South America. By the fifteenth century C.E., they had been living for centuries on the islands of the Caribbean. These islands are located south of the North American mainland. The Arawak were hunters and farmers. The warm climate and plentiful rain allowed them to grow a variety of crops. Corn, beans, sweet

This early Spanish illustration shows Arawak people eating human body parts. However, historians do not have evidence that the Arawak were cannibals. (Library of Congress)

potatoes, peanuts, peppers, cotton, and tobacco grew in abundance. The Arawak also grew manioc (*MAN-ee-oc*). Manioc roots were ground into a pulp and made into a type of bread. Today, manioc is used to make tapioca pudding.

In general, the Arawak were a peaceful people. They went to war only to defend themselves from enemies. They were skilled traders and often had contact with the peoples of South and Central America. They also traded with the Native American nations of the **Florida** (see p. 82) coast. The Arawak exchanged cultural traits along with trade goods. For example, the Arawak had a highly structured society with a powerful chief in each village. The chief made decisions for everyone in times of peace and war. This same type of structure was found among the Aztec and Natchez (*NATCH-ez*) peoples, with whom the Arawak traded. The Arawak were the first native peoples to come into contact with the explorer Christopher Columbus at the end of the 15th century C.E.

Aztec (Mexica)

Mesoamerican civilization. The Aztec were a warlike people who founded a great empire. They were at the height of their power from about 1200 C.E. to about 1500 C.E. when Spanish explorers arrived in their homeland. Their empire stretched from central

Mexico into what is now Guatemala (*gwah-tuh-MAH-luh*).

The Aztec expanded their lands through battles with other **Mesoamerican** (see p. 29) peoples. They demanded taxes from the people in the lands they captured. The taxes included gold, silver, jade, turquoise, and *obsidian*. They also took food products such as corn, beans, tomatoes, chili peppers, mangoes, and papaya. Equally important to the Aztec, they took captives for human sacrifice. Earlier Mesoamerican peoples practiced human sacrifice for their religious rituals. The Aztec did this on a much larger scale. They believed that their gods wanted human blood. They worshiped many gods. Thousands of prisoners were killed at the tops of their temple pyramids.

The emperor was the most powerful ruler in Aztec society. Nobles and priests advised him. The highest classes of Aztec society were served by thousands of soldiers, merchants, farmers, and enslaved peoples. Education was prized among the upper classes. People studied astronomy, painting, and writing. The Aztec used an alphabet of pictures called hieroglyphics (*hy-roh-GLIF-ics*). This alphabet helped them create books of their own history and poetry, and to record public events.

The Aztec were also great builders. They created new land to build on and to farm. The new lands were called *chinampas* (*CHEE-nahm-pas*). The Aztec created the *chinampas* by first securing wicker baskets to the shallow bottom of a lake. Then, they would pile silt and plant matter on top of the baskets. Eventually, they were able to create the *chinampas*, or artificial islands. Over many years, the city of Tenochtitlán (*ten-NOCK-teet-lahn*) was built on top of the *chinampas*. Tenochtitlán was the greatest of the Aztec cities. There were thousands of stone buildings connected by canals that ran throughout the city. When it was at its largest, 300,000 people lived within the city limits. Modern Mexico City is built upon the site of ancient Tenochtitlán.

Celtiberians

Ancient people of the **Iberian Peninsula** (see p. 27). When the **Celts** (see p. 23) crossed the Pyrenees in about 1000 B.C.E., they found the **Iberian** (see p. 27) peoples living there. The Celts defeated the Iberians and then settled among them. Over time, the

Celts and Iberians blended their cultures to create a new people called Celtiberians.

The Celtiberians were warriors like both the Celts and the Iberians. They had many nations, each headed by a warrior chief or king. Their skill as fighters won them respect among the Carthaginians. Carthaginians hired them as paid soldiers in their battles against the Romans from 218 B.C.E. to 210 B.C.E. The Celtiberians valued horses and became excellent mounted soldiers, or cavalry. The Romans eventually used the Celtiberian cavalry in their armies as well.

The Celtiberians were also farmers and herdsmen. They raised small sheep and cattle for food and clothing. Wheat, barley, and corn were used to make bread and a type of beer. The Celtiberians frequently warred among themselves. Over time, they became strong enough for the Romans to consider them a threat to Roman power. There were many Celtiberian tribes. Defeating the smaller tribes made it easier for the Romans to conquer all Celtiberians in 133 B.C.E.

A Roman's View of the Celtiberians

Diodorus Siculus (d. 21 B.C.E.) wrote forty books of world history. He chronicled many of the invasions of the Roman armies up to Caesar's war with the Celtic Gauls. One of his books describes how the Celtiberians came to be.

In ancient times, these two peoples, namely the Iberians and the Celts, kept warring among themselves over the land, but when later they arranged their differences and settled upon the land altogether, and when they went further and agreed to intermarry with each other, because of such intermixture the two peoples received the appellation [Celtiberians] . . . And since it was two powerful nations that united and the land of theirs was fertile, it came to pass that the Celtiberians advanced far in fame.

Celts

Ancient northern and eastern European peoples. The ancient Celts came from the area that is now eastern Europe. By 1000 B.C.E., the early Celts had spread west into the territory north of the Alps Mountains and into the region that has become France. Many Celts settled in this area, which the Romans called Gaul. Around this time, other Celts crossed the Pyrenees into the **Iberian Peninsula** (see p. 27). The invading Celts defeated the **Iberian** (see p. 27) peoples who were living in the area.

Celts were known as fearsome warriors but also as skilled farmers and artisans. There were many nations of Celts, each lead by a king or chief. Their priests were known as Druids (*DRU-ids*). The Druids were considered wise men and keepers of the law. Celts also held singers and poets in high regard. Celtic artists produced intricate jewelry in bronze and gold. Some of their styles were adopted later into Spanish metalwork for brooches and weapons.

The early Celts did not have a written language. Their history was passed down through the generations in the form of spoken histories and songs. The spoken language of the Celts is the basis for the Irish, Welsh, Scottish, and Breton languages of today.

Chavin

Ancient South American civilization. The Chavin peoples were one of the oldest civilizations in what is now Peru. They lived in the highlands of the Andes Mountains from about 850 B.C.E. to 300 B.C.E. The Chavin were farmers and traders who had contact with many other civilizations throughout their area. Chavin de Huantar (*sha-VEEN duh HWAN-tar*) the site of one of the most ancient cities in the Americas. Historians believe that this city was a religious center visited by many different peoples. This contact helped to spread Chavin culture to many places within the Andes.

The Chavin are known for their unusual art. They used methods to create painting and sculpture that had not been used before. The jaguar was often the subject of Chavin art. It is believed that they revered the jaguar as part of their religion. The Chavin peoples also developed new ways of weaving, making pottery, working metal, and growing food.

Like the **Olmec** (see p. 33) in **Mesoamerica** (see p. 29), the Chavin greatly influenced many cultures that came after them. Chavin influence in art and religion can be found among the South American Tiahuanico (*tee-uh-WAN-ee-coh*), **Moche** (*MO-chay*) (see p. 31), Nazca (*NAZ-cuh*), and Chimu (*CHEE-mu*) peoples.

Cid, El (ca. 1043-1099)

Nobleman and military leader. Rodrigo Díaz de Vivar (*rod-REEG-oh DEE-az duh bee-BAR*) was a Castilian (*kath-TIL-yan*) nobleman and general. He had earned the respect of the **Moors** (see p. 31) for his military skill. They gave him the name *Cid*, which means "lord" or "chief." By the middle of the 11th century C.E., southern **Spain** (see p. 39) was breaking into warring Moorish kingdoms. The Christian kings in the north of Spain tried to use this disunity to recapture land. King Alfonso VI of the Spanish kingdom of Castile called upon El Cid to lead the Christian armies against the **Moors** (see p. 31). El Cid captured the important city of Valencia in 1094 C.E. The life of El Cid became a legend that inspired Spanish poetry and literature.

Cordoba

Capital city of Moorish **Spain** (see p. 39). By the beginning of the ninth century C.E., the **Moors** (see p. 31) were firmly established in the southern part of the **Iberian Peninsula** (see p. 27). They made the old Roman city of Cordoba (*cor-DOH-buh*) their capital. Cordoba became one of the most glorious cities in the world.

Cordoba was a city with many marvels. Its streets were paved and lit with street lamps. There were seven hundred mosques (*MAHSKS*)—Muslim houses of worship. About five hundred thousand people lived there and the city offered three hundred public baths for their use. Paper was unknown in most of the Western world, but, in Cordoba, there were bookshops and many libraries. Scholars from all over Europe and the Middle East traveled to Cordoba to study and teach philosophy, science, and medicine. There was free schooling for the poor. The Moors established a society in which Jews, Christians, and Muslims could live and work together.

The great city of Cordoba continued to be prosperous until the beginning of the eleventh century C.E. At this time, the Moorish kingdoms started to break apart. Cordoba fell to several Moorish then Christian armies. By the fifteenth century C.E., Cordoba was once more under Christian rule.

Ferdinand II of Aragon and Isabella I of Castile

Spanish monarchs. In the sixteenth century, **Spain** (see p. 39) became one of the most powerful countries in Europe. The marriage of Ferdinand and Isabella provided the foundation for Spain's success.

Ferdinand and Isabella wave Christopher Columbus on his way. (Library of Congress)

The marriage of Ferdinand II of Aragon (*AIR-uh-gon*) (1452–1516 C.E.) and Isabella I of Castile (*Cath-TEEL*) (1451–1504 C.E.) in 1469 united the two powerful Spanish kingdoms of Aragon and Castile in a political alliance. Ferdinand and Isabella combined their forces to achieve both their goals. One of these goals was the completion of the **Reconquista** (*ray-con-KEES-tuh*) (see p. 37). In 1482, Ferdinand and Isabella's forces occupied Granada, a former Muslim stronghold. It took many years, but they succeeded in driving out the Muslims by 1492.

While the battle for Granada was taking place, the Italian explorer Christopher Columbus asked Queen Isabella for help in his planned voyages. In 1492, Isabella gave Columbus the money he needed to build his fleet. Columbus's explorations resulted in lands in the New World being claimed by Spain as part of Ferdinand and Isabella's empire.

Ferdinand and Isabella's desire for religious unity in Spain led to actions to remove non-Christians from their country. In 1480, the **Inquisition** (*in-KWI-zi-shun*) (see p. 40) had begun (see Spanish Inquisition). In 1492, Jews who would not convert to Christianity were expelled from Spain.

Gibraltar

Peninsula located on Spain's Mediterranean coast. Gibraltar is a very narrow piece of land that has had an important role in the history of **Spain** (see p. 39). Only three miles long and three-quarters of a mile wide, it is connected to Spain by a narrow strip of land with water on each side. Its name honors the Muslim who began the Moorish conquest of Spain in 711 C.E. In Arabic, *Gibraltar* is "Jabal Tariq" (*JAH-bahl tah-REEK*) meaning "Mount Tarik" (*MOWNT tah-REEK*). Tarik Ibn Ziyad (*tah-REEK EE-bin zee-YAHD*) captured Gibraltar and used it as a fortress. By 1501, the **Moors** (see p. 31) had been driven out of Spain. **King Ferdinand and Queen Isabella** (see p. 25) then made Gibraltar part of Spain.

Gibraltar is considered one of the two Pillars of Hercules from Greek mythology. (The other is Ceuta of the African side of the strait.) In ancient times, sea travelers considered Gibraltar the end of the world. Gibraltar is only ten miles across the Mediterranean Sea from the coast of North Africa. This has made it a popular place for invasions from North Africa. The **Iberians** (see p. 27) and Carthaginians both sailed across this narrow strip

The Iberian Peninsula is home to Spain and Portugal.

of the Mediterranean to reach Spain. In the fifth century C.E., the **Vandals** (see p. 40) crossed from Gibraltar to North Africa in their invasion of parts of that continent.

Iberian Peninsula

Geographic area in Europe. The Iberian Peninsula is in the south-western part of what is now Europe. It ranges from the Pyrenees Mountains in the northeast to **Gibraltar** (see p. 26) in the south. The Mediterranean Sea is on its eastern side, while the Atlantic Ocean is on the western and northern side. Spain and Portugal are the two countries that occupy the Iberian Peninsula. Only ten miles separate the southern tip of the peninsula from the coast of North Africa. This has made the peninsula a desirable destination for merchant nations and for peoples migrating from North Africa.

Iberians

Prehistoric people of southern and eastern **Spain** (see p. 39). A nation of peoples crossed into the **Iberian Peninsula** (see p. 27) from North Africa around 3000 B.C.E. They settled the peninsula as far north as the Ebro River. It is from this river that the Iberians get their name.

The Iberians were farmers and warriors who spread throughout the peninsula. They had separate nations, each with its own leader. The Iberians had their own system of writing based on Greek and Phoenician systems. This changed during the time of the Roman conquest of Iberia around 205 B.C.E.

Inca

South American native civilization. The Inca were an advanced and wealthy people who lived in the central Andes Mountains of South America. In about 1200 C.E., the Inca settled in the Cuzco (*COOZ-coh*) valley in what is now Peru. By the 15th century C.E., the Inca Empire stretched from what is now Ecuador to

The Real Home of the Potato

Many people believe the potato arrived in the Americas from Europe. Actually, it was the other way around. The Inca were the first people in the world to grow potatoes. The potatoes that were grown in Europe were of a similar type to the Incan potato.

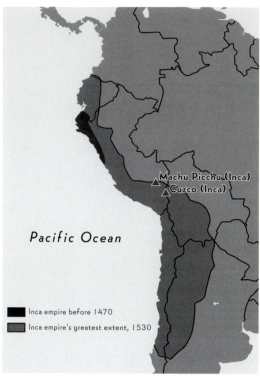

Machu Picchu (Inca)
Cuzco (Inca)

Pacific Ocean

Inca empire before 1470

Inca empire's greatest extent, 1530

The Inca Empire in South America grew quickly between 1470 and 1530. In 1530, the Spanish conquered the empire.

Chile, a distance of about twenty-five hundred miles.

The Inca built a system of roads that covered nearly ten thousand miles. They built sturdy rope suspension bridges across rivers and mountain gorges. The roads were very important for the movement of people and goods. The roads also made communication easier between towns and villages. Along with roads, the Inca built great palaces and temples.

Like the **Mesoamerican** (see p. 29) nations in Central America, the Inca had a society with a very powerful king. The king, nobles, and priests were supported by a much larger group of farmers, merchants, warriors, and craftspeople. The Inca religion revolved around the worship of the sun. The Inca believed their kings were descended directly from the sun god. They also believed gold was the symbol of the sun. The kings and nobility used gold for many things. Skilled craftspeople made gold jewelry, knives, and plates. There were even solid sheets of gold used for the walls of palaces and temples.

The Inca did not have a written language. Instead, they relied on a special group of people called history keepers. The job of the history keepers was to tell the stories about the history of the Inca to each generation. The Inca developed a system of counting using colored strings with knots tied into them. These were called *quipas* (*KWEE-pahs*).

Fertile soil in the lands of Inca Empire permitted farmers to grow a variety of crops. The Inca grew corn, sweet potatoes, cassava, and *quinoa* (*KEEN-wah*). Seeds from the quinoa were used for flour, cereal, and soups. After harvesting the crops, the Inca dried some of the food and stored it in case of war or famine. Horses were not used before the arrival of the European explorers in the sixteenth century. The Inca used llamas instead of horses to carry goods. They also raised *alpaca* for wool, which was woven into clothing and beautiful tapestries.

Maya

Mesoamerican (see p. 29) civilization. The Maya peoples were generally thought to have the most advanced of the Mesoamerican cultures. Their culture flourished from 200 to 1000 C.E. They lived on what is now the Yucatán Peninsula (*YOO-cuh-tan pen-IN-soo-luh*). Like the **Olmec** (see p. 33) before them, the Maya built large pyramids. Many of these pyramids were used as temples or observatories. Mayan cities had palaces, ball courts, and aqueducts, which are systems of pipes that bring water into cities.

The Maya grew a large variety of crops, including *maize*, squash, chili peppers, and beans as well as cotton and cocoa. *Irrigation* canals were used to water the crops. The Maya located on the Gulf shores established trade routes with other cultures in the area. Fish and other seafood were a part of their diet.

The Maya were advanced in astronomy, mathematics, and language. They developed a calendar system, that was nearly as exact as the modern calendar. The Maya knew that the sun was the center of the solar system many years before the Europeans made this discovery. The Maya built observatories to watch the movement of the planets. Mayan astronomers learned to predict eclipses and calculate the cycles of the moon. Their mathematical system was very similar to the decimal system we use today. Even their written language was more complex and exact than those of other Mesoamerican cultures. The Maya greatly influenced all Mesoamerican cultures that came after them. The Maya people were still present in the Yucatán Peninsula when the first Spanish explorers arrived in the sixteenth century.

Mesoamerica

Ancient region that reached from central **Mexico** (see p. 62) through the upper part of Central America. **Mesoamerica** (see p. 29) means "Middle America." Several highly organized civilizations lived in this region from about 2000 B.C.E. until the sixteenth century C.E. The region had the greatest numbers of peoples in the Americas. The Mesoamerican peoples included the **Olmec** (see p. 33), **Maya** (see p. 29), Zapotec (*ZAP-oh-tek*), Mixtec (*MEEKS-tek*), Toltec (*TOL-tek*), Tarascan (*tuh-rahs-KAHN*), and **Aztec** (see p. 20).

High Stakes

Many of the Mesoamerican cultures enjoyed playing a ball game in an enclosed court. Over six hundred ball-playing courts have been discovered in Mexico by **archaeologists**. The Olmecs are given credit for inventing the game. The Olmecs created a rubber ball using extract from the rubber tree. The ball was slightly smaller than the human hand. The object of the game was to gain points by having the ball bounce off certain parts of the court walls. The game could be won by launching the ball through a stone hoop attached to the wall of the ball court. Players could not touch the ball with their hands but could, and did, use other parts of their bodies. They could bounce the ball off knees, elbows, hips—even their heads. Although the players might have fun with this game, sometimes it was deadly serious. To the Olmecs, Maya, and Aztecs, the ball game symbolized the battle between life and death. In ritual games, the captain of the losing team was beheaded.

◀ **archaeologists**
scientists who excavate, or carefully dig out, objects that have been buried in the ground. Archaeologists try to learn about the cultures of people from the past by studying the remains of the ancient objects that belonged to them.

The Mesoamericans built large cities with populations as big as some modern-day cities. For example, one hundred thousand people lived in Teotihuacan (*tee-oh-hwa-h-KAHN*), a city that existed from about 100 B.C.E. to 700 C.E. About two hundred thousand people lived in Tenochtitlán, which existed from 1325 C.E. to 1521 C.E. These cities, and others like them, had small houses and apartment buildings for common people to live in. Many people also lived on farms in outlying areas around the city limits. The kings, priests, and other nobility lived in palaces and temples. These were filled with beautiful artwork. The cities contained large stadiums where sports were played. Some of the Mesoamerican peoples established trade routes through the Sonoran (*son-OR-an*) Desert north of their lands. They traded such items as *obsidian* tools, ceramic vessels, woven cloth, parrot feathers, and copper bells for turquoise and obsidian.

Religion was very important to the Mesoamerican peoples. They believed in many gods and made religious ceremonies central to their way of life. They had celebrations for the change of seasons, for winning at war, even for games of sport. Some of these celebrations involved sacrificing humans to their gods. The people who were killed as offerings to the gods were usually captives taken in battle. Certain wild animals such as eagles and jaguars were especially sacred to the Mesoamericans. To honor these creatures, craftspeople created sculptures and masks made of gold and rare stones. The presence of so much gold drew Spanish explorers to the area. The explorers' desire for the gold and other riches caused them to bring war against and to defeat the Mesoamericans.

Moche

Ancient South American civilization. The Moche (*MO-chay*) lived in what is now northern Peru from about 200 to 700 C.E. They built large, flat-topped pyramids, which were used as temples, palaces, or royal tombs. Their society was made up of several classes. The Moche warrior-priests ruled in their society. The other classes were pottery makers, metalworkers, weavers, farmers, and fishermen.

The Moche grew corn, sweet potatoes, and beans. They used a complex *irrigation* system to bring water to their crops. Fish and game also provided them with food.

The land on which the Moche lived was rich in clay and metal. This made it possible for them to produce beautiful pottery and metal jewelry. Since they did not have a written language, they decorated their pottery with pictures of Moche life. The art of the Moche shows ceremonies, myths, and scenes from everyday life.

Moors

Muslim rulers of **Spain** (see p. 39). In the seventh century C.E., the Islamic religion unified many of the Arab nations. The followers of this religion were called Muslims. Muslim armies swept through the Arabian peninsula and into parts of North Africa. A group of North African *nomads* called Berbers accepted Islam as their religion. In 711 C.E., the Berbers, also called Moors, crossed the Strait of **Gibraltar** (see p. 26) and invaded the **Iberian Peninsula** (see p. 27).

Femme et Fille

A Natchez woman and daughter (Library of Congress)

Tarik ibn Zayid led the Moors into Spain. His armies captured many cities, including **Cordoba** (see p. 24) and Toledo. By 718 C.E., the Moors occupied most of southern Spain. Over the next seven hundred years, the Moors greatly influenced the Spanish character. The Moors brought new ideas in art and literature. They encouraged the study of science and medicine. The great Moorish libraries in Corboda and Toledo preserved ancient Greek and Roman knowledge. Jewish, Muslim, and Christian scholars worked together to teach and learn. By the middle of the tenth century C.E., Spain had become the most civilized country in Europe.

Natchez

Southeastern Native American nation. The Natchez lived from 700 to 1730 C.E. along the lower Mississippi River in what are now the states of Mississippi and Louisiana. The Natchez were one of the cultures referred to as "Mound Builders." The temples, as well as the homes of the king and nobles, were built on the tops of huge earthen mounds. The other people who lived in the village had thatch homes that surrounded the mounds. Mounds were also used as burial sites.

The Natchez culture was strongly influenced by **Mesoamerican** (see p. 29) civilizations such as the **Maya** (see p. 29) and the **Aztec** (see p. 20). Like those cultures, each member of the Natchez nation had a very specific role. The farmers, hunters, soldiers, craftspeople and laborers all worked to support the king and nobles. The king had total power over all the people. The Natchez called their king "the Great Sun." There is one interesting difference between the Natchez peoples and the Mesoamerican cultures: Natchez women who were related to the king or nobles had far more influence in government than high-ranking Mesoamerican women. Among the Natchez, the king's mother acted as his advisor. She had her own home on top of a mound, like the king and nobles. The king's sisters were held in high esteem. They were given honors that many other Native American nations reserved for men.

Navajo

Southwestern Native American nation. The Navajo (*NAH-vuh-ho*) were a nomadic people when they first came to the Southwest about 1025 C.E. The Navajo were made up of bands of hunter-gatherers. They were a fierce people. They raided the **Pueblo** (*PWEB-lo*) (see p. 36) peoples and took food, property, and women. They enslaved many of the people they raided. Over time, the Navajo adopted some of the ways of the peoples who had been their enemies. They learned farming and how to make pottery and baskets.

The Navajo lived in shelters called *hogans* (*HO-guns*). These were usually cone-shaped but sometimes had six or eight sides. The hogan's frame was made of logs and poles and was covered with bark and earth. In later years, the Navajo used stone and adobe. *Adobe* (*ah-DOH-be*) is a type of dried clay. The hogans always were built so that the doorway faced east toward the rising sun.

Art was very important to the Navajo. It had a large influence on their religious ceremonies. They believed that art was a way to communicate with spiritual beings and to be closer to their ancestors. The Navajo became especially skilled at an art called sand painting. Sand painting involves creating temporary designs on the ground with different colored sand particles. This type of art was learned from the **Pueblo** (see p. 36) peoples. The Navajo also created wonderful chants and songs to tell the stories of their people.

Olmec

Mesoamerican nation. The Olmec (*OL-mek*) lived in the lowland jungles, grasslands, and swamps of the Mexican Gulf Coast. They were the largest nation in the area from about 1500 to 300 B.C.E. The Olmec culture influenced many other Mesoamerican cultures that came after it. These included the **Maya** (see p. 29), **Aztec** (see p. 20), Toltec (*TOL-tek*), and Zapotec (*ZAP-oh-tek*).

The Olmec were the first Mesoamerican culture to have defined classes of people. The classes included merchants, craftspeople, and priests. The priests had the most power in Olmec society. There were also classes of farmers and fisherpeople. A person was born into one of these classes and could not move from one class to another.

Large Olmec villages grew to be centers of trade and religious ceremony. It was within these communities that the merchants, craftspeople, and priests lived. Their homes were made of stone and were located along paved streets. Some of these homes were temples on the tops of pyramids. A system of stone pipes was built to supply them with water from outside the city. The farmers lived on the land surrounding the community. The farmers and fisherpeople supported the upper classes. The Olmec grew corn, beans, peppers, and pumpkins. They also ate wild game, fish, and other seafood.

Jaguars and a plumed serpent called Quetzalcoatl (*ket-suh-KAH-tuhl*) were important figures in Olmec religion. The Olmec believed these gods demanded blood as a sacrifice. Human and animal sacrifice was a part of their religious rituals. The Olmec are famous for the huge sculptures of their gods and of human heads. The sculptures were carved out of basalt (*buh-SALT*), a dark volcanic rock. Some of these sculptures are ten feet tall and weigh twenty tons. The Olmec were the first Mesoamerican people to have a number system. They were also the first to understand the concept of zero, to develop a complex and accurate calendar, and to create a written language that used pictures and symbols.

Phoenicians

Ancient Mediterranean peoples. The Phoenicians (*fuh-NEE-shuns*) were ancient Middle-Eastern peoples. They were famous sea travelers, explorers, and merchants. The Phoenicians developed boats with *keeled* hulls, which allowed them to sail in the deeper waters of the Mediterranean Sea.

In approximately 3000 B.C.E., the Phoenicians settled along the coast of what is now Lebanon. They built seaports in places where the trading routes on land and on sea came together. The ports allowed the Phoenicians to trade with peoples in North Africa, **Spain** (see p. 39), India, and many other nations. They traded such items as cedar, fine linen, glass, wine, ivory, silk, spices, and different metals. Tin was a prized metal in the world of the Phoenicians. While looking for sources of tin, the Phoenicians made their way to what is now Spain. They founded the cities of Tarshish (*tar-SHEESH*) and Cádiz (*cad-EEZ*) on the coast of Spain. These became great trading cities. They also founded the city of Carthage on the coast of North Africa.

The Phoenicians were the first to discover how to use the North Star to help them stay on course while sailing. They were the first people to sail all the way around Africa.

The Phoenician alphabet was made up of twenty-two consonants. This alphabet is the foundation of the English alphabet we use today.

Portugal

Southwestern European country. Portugal (*PORT-chu-gul*) is located on the western coast of the **Iberian Peninsula** (see p. 27). For most of its early history, Portugal and **Spain** (see p. 39) were considered one nation. In the tenth and eleventh centuries C.E., northern Portugal was recaptured from the **Moors** (see p. 31). It became a Spanish state. In 1139, Count Alfonso Henriques (*en-REE-kays*) declared that Portugal was independent from Spain. He became Portugal's first king.

King Alfonso (al-FAHN-so) recaptured even more territory from the Moors. By the fifteenth century C.E., Portugal became Spain's rival in trade and exploration. By 1419 C.E., Prince Henry of Portugal had sent many ships to explore the coast of Africa. In 1450, Prince Henry established the first school to teach sailors navigation methods and mapmaking. By 1452, Portuguese explorers had established trade with some West African nations. Some of this trade involved the exchange of enslaved peoples.

The Portuguese continued to be great explorers and sailors. In 1488 C.E., Bartholomeu Dias (*bar-TAHL-oh-MAY-oo DEE-as*) sailed around the Cape of Good Hope, which is on the southern tip of Africa. This allowed traders to reach the trading centers of India

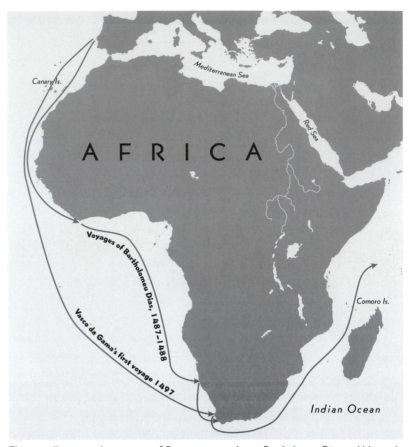

This map illustrates the voyages of Portuguese explorers Bartholomeu Dias and Vasco da Gama. Dias was the first European to explore the West Afrcian Coast south to the Cape of Good Hope in Southern Africa.

by sea. Portuguese explorers were the first Europeans to see the continent of Australia. Throughout the sixteenth century C.E., Portugal established many colonies. These colonies were in Brazil, West Africa, India, Japan, and China. Even though Brazil is in South America, it is not considered part of Hispanic America. This is because Portuguese, not Spanish, is spoken in Brazil.

Pueblo

Southwestern Native American nation. The Pueblo nation was made up of many different nations. The Hopi (*HO-pee*) lived in what is now Arizona. The Zuñi (*ZOO-nee*) made their home in what is now eastern New Mexico. The other Pueblo peoples lived along a 130-mile stretch of the Rio Grande River. They were the Tigua (*TEE-gwuh*), the Tewa (*TEE-wuh*), the Jemez (*HEE-mez*), and the Keres (*KARE-ez*).

A Pueblo village (Library of Congress)

The Pueblo were excellent farmers and raised several different crops. These included cotton, tobacco, beans, squash, and corn. The hunters of the community went after deer, antelope, and rabbits. The Pueblo women were skilled at weaving baskets and making pottery, which they polished and painted with beautiful designs.

The dwellings in which the Pueblo lived were unusual among Native American structures. These structures, known as pueblos, had up to five levels. They looked something like a modern-day apartment building. The flat roof of the lower level was the floor and front yard of the level above it. The Pueblo built these dwellings without doors and windows on the bottom level to make it more difficult for enemies to attack. This also made it impossible for the people who lived in the lower levels to get to their homes. The Pueblo solved this problem by creating an entrance that was a hole in the floor of the next level up. The residents of the lower dwellings descended into the lower levels of their homes through these holes.

Reconquista

A series of military actions by Spanish and Portuguese Christian nations to recapture territory from the **Moors** (see p. 31). The Moors successfully invaded **Spain** (see p. 39) in 711 C.E. By the middle of the eighth century, the Moors controlled most of south-

Ruins of a Roman theater in Spain (Library of Congress)

ern Spain. As early as 718 C.E., the Christian kingdoms to the north and west of the Moorish territory attempted to take back territory they had lost. It started with the Battle of Covadonga. This battle stopped the Moorish advance. However, the Reconquista didn't make real progress until the eleventh century C.E. By this time, the Moorish kingdoms had become weaker. By the middle of the thirteenth century C.E., much of the land had been recaptured. The Reconquista was completed in the fifteenth century C.E. when the Moorish city of Granada was captured by Christian forces.

Rome

Ancient city. For almost eight hundred years, the city of Rome was the home of the most powerful nation in the world. From the late third century B.C.E. until the fifth century C.E., Roman civilization touched other cultures throughout the known world. In 117 C.E., the Roman Empire controlled most of western Europe, large areas of North Africa, and the area known as the Mediterranean basin. Roman power rested on its powerful and disciplined army. Once the army captured territory, the real Roman work began.

The Romans influenced the people they conquered in many ways. The Romans had a formal collection of laws that were enforced in all areas of the empire. The Roman language, Latin, is the basis for modern Spanish, Italian, Portuguese and French. The Romans built roads throughout their conquered lands to make trade and communication easier. Many of these roads still exist today. The Romans also adopted knowledge and traditions of the native peoples they controlled. Much of ancient Greek civilization was saved and passed on in this way.

Around 205 C.E., the Romans invaded the **Iberian Peninsula** (see p. 27). They controlled the area that would become **Spain** (see p. 39) and **Portugal** (see p. 35) for over six hundred years. They gave Spain law, language, and roads that remained after the Romans left. Over the centuries, cities that the Romans founded, such as **Cordoba** (see p. 24) and Seville, became great places of beauty and learning.

Rome continued to be a powerful presence in Spain and western Europe even after the Roman Empire fell. Rome became the religious center of the Roman Catholic Church. This Church and the popes who led it were an important influence on the kings and queens of Europe. The popes encouraged the Spanish and Portuguese kings and queens to explore unknown lands. To millions of Roman Catholics today, Rome is still a center of great power and influence.

Spain

Southwestern European country. Spain is located on a peninsula in the southwestern tip of Europe. The peninsula is known as the **Iberian Peninsula** (see p. 27). Spain shares the peninsula with the country of **Portugal** (see p. 35).

Spain is located at the place where Europe and Africa almost meet. Both the Mediterranean Sea and the Atlantic Ocean border it. The ancient Greeks believed that Spain was at the western end of the known world. Despite this, its location made it a desirable place for trade. It also made it easy to invade. Spain's coastline on the Mediterranean Sea provided ports for ships. Greeks, Romans, **Phoenicians** (see p. 34), North Africans, and Islamic peoples all took advantage of these ports. These people brought their own traditions and beliefs.

From the arrival of the **Iberians** (see p. 27) in 3000 B.C.E. to the invasion of the **Moors** (see p. 31) in 711 C.E., Spain has been like a blanket made of many different fabrics and colors. The

Spanish character has been affected by Roman, Germanic, Christian, and Muslim traditions. It is the only country in Europe that experienced so many different influences over its history. Spain used all of these influences as it moved into the fifteenth century C.E. and the Age of Exploration.

Spain led the world during the Age of Exploration. The first voyage of **Christopher Columbus** (see p. 52) in 1492 C.E. began Spain's journeys to the Americas. Spain increased its lands in the Americas throughout the sixteenth century. Spaniards explored vast areas of what is now Central and Latin America. They established colonies in the southwest areas of North America. The Spanish influenced the language, traditions, and government in all of these places. Because of this, Spain is considered to be one of the main contributors to today's Hispanic American culture.

Spanish Inquisition

Attempt to force religious unity in **Spain** (see p. 39). In fifteenth-century Spain, people who did not believe in the Roman Catholic faith were considered enemies of society. **Queen Isabella and King Ferdinand** (see p. 25) wanted to unite Spain's peoples under one government and one religion. They became allies of Pope Sixtus IV and began a series of investigations to find those who didn't believe in the Catholic faith. A Dominican friar named Tomas de Torquemada led the investigations.

Torquemada used torture to get people to confess to being enemies of the state. About two thousand people were burned at the stake during the years that Torquemada led the Spanish Inquisition. Most of these people were Jews or Muslims. Many of these were *conversos*.

The Spanish Inquisition began in 1478 C.E. It continued in various forms in the New World and parts of Europe until the early years of the nineteenth century.

Vandals

Germanic people. The Vandals settled in **Spain** (see p. 39) in 409 C.E. after escaping their enemies. They were only in Spain for a short time before they moved to North Africa in 429 C.E. They established a kingdom there and became allies of the Roman

Empire. In 435 C.E., they betrayed their Roman allies and captured the Roman-controlled city of Carthage in North Africa. The Vandals set up their own kingdom. Over the following twenty years, they captured some of the islands located off the coast of Italy. In 455 C.E., the Vandals attacked **Rome** (see p. 38) itself. The Vandals burned the city and stole many works of art. The word *vandalism* comes from the actions of the Vandal people.

Visigoths

Germanic nation. The Visigoths came from the area now known as Romania. In 376 C.E., they started to travel into parts of the Roman Empire. In 410 C.E., they attacked **Rome** (see p. 38). The Visigoths' success against the Romans allowed other Germanic tribes such as the **Vandals** (see p. 40), Alan (*AL-ahn*), and Suevi (*SWAY-vi*) to move into **Spain** (see p. 39). The Romans asked the Visigoths to become allies and to drive out the other Germanic people. The Visigoths agreed and, in 415 C.E., the Visigoths settled into the area that became France.

In 466 C.E., the Visigoths drove the Suevi and Alan peoples out of Spain and established a kingdom of their own. They made the city of Toledo in Spain their capital.

The Visigoths kept much of Roman law and customs while adding some of their own Germanic traditions. They also converted to Christianity. The Visigoths held Toledo until the **Moors** (see p. 31) invaded in 711 C.E. The Visigoths were pushed out of Toledo and retreated to the far northern part of Spain. The Visigothic kings began the **Reconquista** (see p. 37) in 718 C.E.

West Africa

Nations of western Africa. Like **Spain** (see p. 39), Africa has had a long and complex history. It is a large continent with thousands of different peoples. Each area has its own story. In West Africa, the story includes the arrival of Muslim traders from North Africa and explorers from the European continent.

The kingdoms of West Africa are considered sub-Saharan (*sub-suh-HAR-an*). This means that they are located south of the Sahara Desert. For centuries, the Sahara Desert acted as a barrier to invasion of sub-Saharan areas by peoples from North Africa and the Middle East. By the fifth century C.E., this had changed.

Ghana (*GAHN-uh*) was the most powerful kingdom in West Africa from the fifth through the twelfth centuries C.E. The nation of Ghana controlled the trade routes through the Sahara Desert. The people of Ghana grew wealthy in the trade of gold and slaves for goods from the North African and Middle Eastern lands. Ghana remained powerful until the beginning of the thirteenth century C.E..

The Kingdom of Mali (*MAH-lee*) was home to the Mandinka (*man-DINK-uh*) people. They had been in West Africa since the eleventh century C.E. but did not become the most powerful nation until the fourteenth century C.E. During this time, the Kingdom of Mali reached more than one thousand miles across West Africa. It continued the trade begun by the Kingdom of Ghana. In the early part of the fourteenth century C.E., the Kingdom of Songhai rose to become the most powerful. Each of these kingdoms depended on the trade from merchants traveling through the Sahara Desert. In the beginning of the fifteenth century C.E., a new source of trade appeared.

In 1439, Portuguese explorers arrived on the coast of West Africa. This provided a new way to trade—by sea rather than through the desert. There were many West African kingdoms along the coast that were anxious to trade with the Portuguese and others who came after them. The Kingdom of Benin (*ben-EEN*) in what is now Nigeria was famous for beautiful bronze sculptures. The Yoruba (*yoh-RU-buh*) people of the Oyo Kingdom in Nigeria also became a large source of trade for the Portuguese and others.

Not all of the West African peoples were part of large and powerful nations. The Ibo and the Tiv people of Nigeria lived in smaller villages. They had a council of elders that governed how the people lived. Often, the people in a village were close relatives.

The arrival of the Portuguese and other explorers forever changed the lives of all West African peoples. The explorers and traders influenced traditions and beliefs that had been handed down for generations. The increasing demand for slaves affected all the West African peoples who came into contact with the explorers who had sailed to Africa.

CHAPTER TWO

The Spanish Empire

Spain in the Americas, 1492–1775

"Gazing on such wonderful sights we did not know what to say or whether what appeared before us was real."

—Spanish conquistador, after seeing Tenochtitlán, the Aztec capital.

At the beginning of the 16th century, three very different worlds were about to come together. They would join in a place called the Americas. There, peoples from Europe, Africa, and the American continents would meet. Each nation of peoples would in some way influence the others.

In 1492, an Italian explorer, **Christopher Columbus** (see p. 52), set sail for India. He sailed on ships given to him by the king and queen of Spain (see **Ferdinand II of Aragon and Isabella I of Castile**, p. 25). The voyage took much longer than he expected. After many months, he saw land. The land was an island. He was happy because he thought the island was part of India.

When Columbus and his crew went ashore, the people who lived on the island greeted them. Columbus and his men had never before seen people like this. The island-dwellers had brown skin and wore very little clothing. They wore gold jewelry. Friendly and welcoming, they brought food and gifts for the men who had arrived on the giant ships. Columbus thought these people were from India so he called them "Indians."

The people were not Indians. They were the **Arawak** (*AIR-uh-wak*) (see p. 19). The Arawak were a Native American people. The island was not part of India. It was actually an island in the Caribbean (*cuh-RIB-ee-un* or *care-uh-BE-un*) Sea. Columbus had not known this sea and island existed. Two peoples came together for the first time, and the history of Spanish America began.

Christopher Columbus and his men come ashore in the Bahamas. (Library of Congress)

The Arawak did not know that these newcomers were going to claim Arawak land for some distant and unknown nation called **Spain** (see p. 39). They did not know that Columbus would eventually enslave them. They did not know that he was hungry for gold. They certainly did not know that

Timeline

1492

Christopher Columbus commands his first voyage to find a trade route to India. He reaches an island in what is now the Bahamas. He calls it "San Salvador" and claims it for Spain. His reports of the voyage open the door for Spanish exploration in the New World.

1508

Juan Ponce de León conquers Puerto Rico.

Columbus's arrival had opened the gates to their world. Soon, many more explorers would pass like a flood over the Native American peoples.

Between 1492 and 1504, Columbus made four voyages to the islands in the Caribbean Sea. During those visits, the Arawak were enslaved. Their land was taken from them. Peoples on other islands in the Caribbean met the same fate. By 1496, Columbus had found the island he called Hispaniola (*HISS-pan-ee-oh-luh*). He built a settlement there. The native peoples on Hispaniola also were enslaved.

More and more of the invaders arrived. Many of these men had come to stay. They built houses and farms. They forced the island peoples to work in the mines the invaders had found. They forced the native peoples to give up their religion and way of life. The Native American peoples were forced to accept a religion called Christianity that was new to them.

It did not take long for Columbus's reports of the lands he had found to lead other men to the *New World*. These men, called **conquistadors** (*kon-KEES-tuh-dors*) (see p. 54) were looking for wealth and fame. They also wanted to spread their religion. By 1508, **Juan Ponce de León** (see p. 69) (*wahn PONZ duh lay-OWN*) had conquered the island of Puerto Rico. In 1509, he went on to conquer and settle the island of Jamaica. By 1513, the Spanish had established a colony on the island they named Cuba.

Everywhere the Spanish conquistadors went in the Caribbean, they brought sorrow to the Native American peoples. The strangers brought illness

1509	**1513**	**1521**	**1528**
Juan Ponce de León establishes settlements on the Caribbean island of Jamaica.	**Vasco Nuñez de Balboa** crosses the Isthmus of Panama. He becomes the first European to see the Pacific Ocean from the western coast of South America.	**Juan Ponce de León** tries to establish a colony in **Florida**. The Calusa fight the invaders. Ponce de Léon is wounded and dies shortly afterward. **Hernán Cortés** completes the conquest of **Mexico**. The Aztec Empire falls.	**Pánfilo de Narváez** leads an expedition to explore the **Florida** coastline. **Álvar Núñez Cabeza de Vaca** and three others from the de Narváez expedition land on the coast of Texas. They begin an eight-year journey through the unexplored southwest part of North America.

and bloodshed. They also brought a belief that they had every right to take what they wanted from all the native peoples in the Americas.

Although some Spanish, such as the priests **Bartolomé de Las Casas** (*bar-TAHL-oh-may duh las KAHS-uhs*) (see p. 60) and **Eusebio Francisco Kino** (*yu-SAY-be-oh fran-SEES-koh KEE-noh*) (see p. 59) spoke out against cruelty toward Native Americans, the Spanish explorers and colonists believed what they were doing was right. They believed the Spanish culture was the best in the world. They felt they had an obligation to spread the Spanish culture and Christianity among all the Native American peoples. Sixteenth-century Spain had its own history of intolerance for other peoples and religions. The **Reconquista** (*ray-con-KEES-tuh*) (see p. 37) and the **Spanish Inquisition** (see p. 40) had driven thousands of **Moors** (see p. 31) and Jews from Spain. This harsh treatment of people within the country's own borders strongly influenced the character of the Spanish conquistadors. These events set the standard for Spain's harsh treatment of peoples in the lands it conquered.

The Spanish invaders tortured and killed many of the native peoples in the *New World*. They enslaved many more. Compared to the cruelty, though, the illness the Spanish conquerors brought proved worst of all. The Spanish and other Europeans introduced deadly diseases to the Native Americans. The native peoples had no natural resistance to these diseases. Smallpox, typhus, and measles swept through the Native American popula-

1532	**1534–1536**	**1534–1536**	**1535**
Francisco Pizarro begins the conquest of Peru.	**Álvar Núñez Cabeza de Vaca, Estéban**, and two others walk from what is now Galveston, Texas, to the west coast of Mexico. They travel through **New Mexico** and Arizona. Native American people they meet tell stories of seven rich cities located somewhere to the north.	Pedro de Mendóza founds Buenos Aires in Argentina.	**Francisco Pizarro** founds a new capital of Peru. He calls the city "Ciudad de los Reyes." It becomes known as Lima.

tions like a fire that destroys everything in its path.

Within fifty years of Columbus's arrival, the populations of Native American peoples of the Caribbean were almost completely destroyed. In 1542, the Spanish priest, Bartolomé de Las Casas wrote: "All those islands . . . are now abandoned and desolate." Most of the native peoples on the Caribbean islands were gone. Although the native peoples of the Caribbean were gone, Las Casas spoke out against the way they had been treated in the hope that other Native Americans would be treated better.

Hernán Cortés (Library of Congress)

The Spanish still needed laborers to work the colonies' mines and farms. The conquistadors began to journey further west in search of gold and laborers. In 1521, **Hernán Cortés** (see p. 55) completed his conquest of **Mexico** (see p. 62) and the **Aztec** (see p. 20) peoples who lived there. By 1535, **Francisco Pizzaro** (see p. 68) in South America had defeated the mighty **Inca** (see p. 27) peoples from Peru. In 1540, the Spanish had reached the territories north of Mexico. **Francisco Vásquez de Coronado** (see p. 54) explored much of the southwest territory of North America. **Hernando de Soto** (see p. 56) explored

1540

Francisco Vasquéz de Coronado searches for the Seven Cities of Cíbola. While searching, he explores California, Arizona, **New Mexico**, Texas, Oklahoma, and Kansas.

1541

Hernando de Soto explores the Mississippi River and the coast of the Gulf of Mexico.

1542

The work of **Bartolomé de Las Casas** results in the New Laws. These prohibit enslavement of Native Americans. Restrictions to the *encomienda* (see *encomendero*, p. 57) system begin.

1588

Spanish Armada is destroyed after many battles with England's fleet under Sir Francis Drake.

the lands along the Mississippi and the coast of the Gulf of Mexico. In all cases, their weapons and diseases helped the Spanish conquer the native peoples.

Before long, Spain had claimed more territory in the **New World** than any other European nation. In 1600, this territory stretched from what is now Chile all the way north along the west coast of South America, throughout Central America, and up into a large part of North America. They called this empire **New Spain** (see p. 67).

As more colonists arrived, there was a greater and greater demand for laborers. The Spanish enslaved many Native Americans who had not already died from disease. Yet, more workers were needed. The Spanish conquerors found those workers in enslaved Africans.

In the middle of the sixteenth century, the Spanish began to import enslaved Africans to work in Spanish settlements. These enslaved laborers were forced to work at a variety of tasks. They worked on the sugar plantations in the Caribbean and in the silver mines of Mexico. Some of the enslaved Africans did skilled metalworking for the Spanish. Others worked to build new houses and churches.

As New Spain grew, so did the ranks of the enslaved. During the seventeenth century, Spain brought over 292,000 enslaved Africans to the Americas. Between 1701 and 1810, that number increased to 600,000 human beings. The Africans were treated as cruelly as the Native Americans had been. To the Spanish, they were possessions, like chairs or horses. The

1595	1598	1640	1680
Spanish forces in the El Morro fortress successfully defend Puerto Rico from attack by English privateers Sir Francis Drake and Sir John Hawkins.	Juan de Oñate founds San Juan de los Caballeros near present-day Santa Fe, **New Mexico**. His poor treatment of the **Pueblo** peoples angers them.	England takes control of the Spanish colony in the Bahamas in the Caribbean. This breaks the Spanish hold on the Caribbean Islands.	Years of mistreatment by the Spanish cause the **Pueblo** nation to revolt (see **Pueblo Revolt**, p. 70). Popé, a Tewa shaman, leads the Hopi, Zuñi, and Acoma peoples in an attack on Santa Fe. Four hundred Spanish are killed. The **Pueblo** hold Santa Fe for more than 10 years.

A typical Spanish mission (Library of Congress)

Spanish relied on the labor of enslaved workers to create the wealth for which they had come to the colonies.

Even though the Spanish treated them harshly, the Spanish culture was greatly affected by both the Native American and African peoples. Many Spanish colonists married Native Americans. Their children became the foundation for a new mixed race of people called **mestizo** (*mes-TEES-os*) (see p. 62). By the beginning of the nineteenth century, many of the people in New Spain were mestizo.

1692	1697	1752	1763
Spanish recapture Santa Fe from the **Pueblo** peoples. **Father Eusebio Francisco Kino** founds Jesuit **missions** among the Yaqui, Yuma, and Pima (see **Akimel O'odham**, p. 19) peoples in Arizona and **New Mexico**.	Spain transfers ownership to France of the western part of Hispaniola. This becomes Haiti.	The Spanish build a presidio at Tubac in Arizona. This is the location of the first permanent European settlement in Arizona.	Spain gains from France the **Louisiana Territory**, which stretches from the Mississippi River to the Rocky Mountains.

The Spanish and African races also intermarried. This was particularly true in the Caribbean colonies of Cuba and Hispaniola. New, blended cultures started to grow throughout Central America, the Caribbean, South America, and the southwestern part of North America. In each place, Spanish traditions and ways of life blended with those of the native peoples. Over time, these blended cultures could not be distinguished from each other. The combined traditions and ways of life created what would become the Hispanic character.

By the eighteenth century, Spanish colonies existed throughout the Americas. There were many towns and **missions** (see p. 64). The conquistadors had been replaced by their descendents. New colonists arrived from Spain to seek their fortunes. Many of the people who lived in the colonies had been born there. Local forms of government had been established. The colonies had learned how to manage their own wealth and resources. They had developed economies. Soon, they no longer wanted to be a part of Spain. The colonies wanted to be separate and independent nations.

In the late eighteenth and early nineteenth centuries, many of the Spanish colonies broke away from Spanish control. Spain was weakening. It had spent large amounts of money on too many European wars. Its own economy was not as strong as it had once been. As the colonies fought for their independence, Spain could not stop them. Three hundred years of Spanish rule in the Americas was coming to an end. Hispanic America was being born.

1769

Father **Junipero Serra** founds the first Franciscan **mission** in California. It is called San Diego.

1770–1781

Father **Junipero Serra** founds **missions** along the California coast at Carmel, San Francisco, Santa Clara, and Los Angeles.

A-Z of Key People, Places and Terms

Balboa, Vasco Núñez de (1475-1519)

Spanish explorer and **conquistador** (*kon-KEES-tuh-dor*) (see p. 54). In 1500 C.E., Vasco Núñez de Balboa (*VAHS-koh noon-YEZ duh bal-BO-uh*) joined a voyage of exploration. It took him to the northern coast of South America to what is now Colombia. In 1510, he started a colony in Darien on the coast of the *isthmus* (*ISS-muss*) of present-day Panama. Seeking wealth, Balboa organized expeditions to look for gold and slaves. He hoped that by trading with Native Americans he could persuade them to help him find gold and slaves. If trade was unsuccessful, he used torture and fear. In 1513, Balboa led an expedition across the narrowest part of the isthmus. He passed through dense jungles and swamps and reached the shores of a vast body of water. Thus, Balboa became the first European to see the Pacific Ocean from the west coast of South America. He returned to his settlement after his discovery. In 1518, Balboa was falsely accused of treason against **Spain** (see p. 39). He was found guilty and was beheaded in January 1519.

Vasco Núñez de Balboa
(Library of Congress)

Cabeza de Vaca, Álvar Núñez (ca.1490–ca.1560)

Spanish explorer. In 1527, Álvar Núñez Cabeza de Vaca (*al-VAR NOON-yez cuh-BAY-zuh duh VAH-kuh*) joined a Spanish expedition to **Florida** (see p. 58). His ship was blown off course. It landed on the Gulf coast of Florida. After many hardships on land, only a few of the crew remained. They tried to sail to Cuba on rafts. Instead, hurricanes forced them to the coast of **Texas** (see p. 91). Native Americans captured Cabeza de Vaca and the other survivors. Cabeza de Vaca escaped into the desert. He wandered through the desert for five years before he was again captured. He

Cabeza de Vaca (front), with Estéban (left), and others (National Park Service)

and three other men escaped again. They were the first Europeans to travel through what is now Texas and northern **Mexico** (see p. 62). They were also the first Europeans to see bison. They met many Native Americans in their travels. After three years, they finally made contact with a Spanish settlement in what is now northern Mexico. Cabeza de Vaca told stories about the riches of seven cities he had seen in his travels. His reports spurred on the explorer **Francisco Vásquez de Coronado** (*fran-SEES-koh vahs-KEZ duh kor-uh-NAHD-oh*) (see p. 54) to begin searching for those "lost" cities.

Columbus, Christopher (1451–1506)

Explorer and navigator. Christopher Columbus was an Italian sailor. He believed he could find a fast route to the trade markets of China and India. His route would be westward across the Atlantic Ocean. If he could do this, it would mean great wealth for Columbus and his sponsors. He approached **King Ferdinand II of Aragon and Queen Isabella I of Castile** (see p. 25), the rulers of **Spain** (see p. 39), with his idea. They agreed to support the expedition. On August 3, 1492, Columbus set sail. He commanded three ships: the *Niña*, the *Pinta*, and the *Santa Maria*. He sailed much farther than he had planned. In October, Columbus finally reached land. He stepped ashore on an island in the

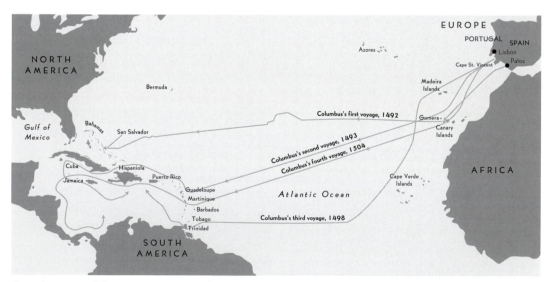

Over the course of four voyages across the Atlantic, Christopher Columbus explored most of the Caribbean and reached as far west as the coast of Central America.

The Columbian Exchange

The exchange of biological species between the Old World and the New World. The Old World describes all the lands east of a certain point on the globe. The people in the Old World believed that the lands they knew of were the only lands on Earth. The discoveries of the fifteenth-century explorers changed this view. The lands that the explorers found were called the New World. The Old and New Worlds contained different types of plants and animals. The diseases in each world were also different. When Christopher Columbus made contact with the Arawak peoples on the island of San Salvador, there began an exchange of plants, animals, and diseases between the two worlds. This is called the Columbian exchange.

Before the arrival of Europeans, Native Americans did not have many farm animals. Cattle, sheep, chickens, horses, donkeys, pigs, and goats were introduced to the New World by explorers and settlers. The native peoples in South America did raise guinea pigs for food. The Columbian exchange introduced the guinea pig to the Old World, where it became a pet.

Along with farm animals, many foods were part of the Columbian exchange. Native peoples in the Americas introduced explorers to cashews, cranberries, peanuts, potatoes, peppers, tomatoes, avocados, maize (corn), and cacao (the source of chocolate). Settlers from the Old World brought with them apples, olives, peaches, wheat, rice, sugar, coffee, grapes, and bananas.

Unfortunately, not everything that was exchanged was good. Certain animals and weeds were shipped across the ocean by mistake. Rats came from the Old World, and dandelions were sent to the New World as well. For the most part, Native Americans did not have alcohol; they were introduced to alcohol by the European explorers. Tobacco and coca, the source of cocaine, were brought to the Old World from the New.

Old World diseases were especially deadly to the native peoples of the Americas. Illnesses such as smallpox, measles, malaria, influenza, typhus, and diphtheria caused many deaths among the Native Americans. They did not have any natural resistance to these diseases. When the Spanish arrived in Mexico around 1519, there were about twenty-five million Native Americans. By the 1620s, there were only one million Native Americans left. Diseases the Spanish brought from the Old World were the cause of most of the deaths. Native peoples in other parts of North and South America experienced similar disasters. It is believed that the disease syphilis (*SIF-ill-iss*) was passed from the New World to the Old. Columbus's crewmembers brought the disease to Europe when they returned from their expeditions.

Bahamas. He named the island "San Salvador."

A friendly, gentle group of native peoples greeted Columbus and his crew. These people were the **Arawak** (see p. 19). They brought parrots, cotton, and wooden spears as gifts for the visitors. Columbus believed he was in India, so he called the Arawak "Indians." Columbus noticed that some of the Arawak were wearing gold. He decided there must be a great deal of gold close by. Columbus went to other islands in the Caribbean looking for this gold. He went to Cuba and Hispaniola. Hispaniola is now Haiti and the Dominican Republic. Columbus did not find the great quantities of gold he had hoped to find. When he returned to Spain, he brought with him some Arawak captives. He presented these people as gifts to Ferdinand and Isabella.

Columbus made three more voyages to the Caribbean. He established settlements but continued to look for the gold he was sure was hidden somewhere on the islands. He continued to enslave many of the native peoples he found on the islands.

Columbus's discovery of the islands opened the way for other explorers to follow. Soon, many would make their own voyages to the Americas. The conquest of the *New World* had begun.

conquistador

Spanish military leader. *Conquistador*, or "conqueror," is the name given to a sixteenth-century leader of the Spanish conquest of the Americas. Conquistadors were men seeking adventure and wealth. They gained these things through battles and bloodshed. **Hernán Cortés** (see p. 55) in **Mexico** (see p. 62), **Francisco Pizarro** (see p. 68) in Peru, and **Vasco Núñez de Balboa** (see p. 51) are examples of famous conquistadors.

Coronado, Francisco Vásquez de (1510–1554)

Spanish explorer and **conquistador** (see above). In 1540, Francisco Vásquez de Coronado led an *expedition* from **Mexico** (see p. 63) in search of the mythical Seven Cities of Cíbola. His expedition took him through areas of present-day Arizona, **New Mexico** (see p. 66), **Texas** (see p. 91), Oklahoma, and Kansas. Coronado and his expedition found the magnificent Grand Canyon and the Colorado River. However, he failed in his search for the treasure he thought existed. The Seven

Coronado and his men search the American Southwest for the Seven Cities of Cíbola. (Library of Congress)

Cities of Cíbola were actually the adobe (*ah-DOH-be*) villages of the Zuñi.

Cortés, Hernán (1485–1547)

Explorer and conqueror of the **Aztec** (see p. 20). Hernán Cortés was an ambitious and clever soldier. He had been on various *expeditions* to the *New World*. The conquest of **Mexico** (see p. 62) and the rich Aztec Empire became his most important goal. In 1519, Cortés landed in the Yucatán with 11 ships, 500 soldiers, 12 muskets, 14 cannons, and many horses and *war dogs*. To make sure that his army could not leave, he burned the ships. On his way to attacking the Aztec Empire, Cortés captured the town of Tabasco. He also founded the city that would become present-day Veracruz (vayr-uh-CROOZ) in Mexico. Cortés then set out to achieve his dream. He went in search of the Aztec. His motto was "To conquer the land or die."

The Aztec nation was very powerful. It was made up of millions of people, many of whom were experienced warriors. It seemed that Cortés did not have a chance against such a strong force. Cortés, however, used his intelligence to defeat the Aztec. Although powerful, the Aztec Empire had problems of its own. Many of the peoples the Aztec had conquered hated them. Cortés used this hatred to gain support for his war against the Aztec. Cortés also used the Aztec's fear of some of the things Cortés carried with him. The Aztec had never seen weapons like those Cortés used. The weapons were loud and destroyed things from a distance. The Aztec also had never seen horses or fierce war

Cortés's army (at left) faces off against Aztec warriors. (Library of Congress)

dogs. All of these things made them weaker in the face of Cortés's attacks.

Cortés tricked the Aztec emperor, Montezuma (*mohn-tuh-ZOO-muh*), and captured him. He made Montezuma promise to support the Spanish. The Aztec eventually killed Montezuma because he seemed to be controlled by Cortés. In 1520, the Aztec tried to destroy Cortés and his soldiers. Aztec warriors succeeded in killing most of the Spanish force, but some escaped. Cortés raised a new army and received some unexpected help.

The Aztec were suffering from smallpox, a disease brought to the *New World* by the Spanish explorers. The Aztec king died along with many others. This made it easier for Cortés to attack their main city of Tenochtitlán (*tuh-NOCK-teet-lahn*). This time, Cortés won. He burned Tenochtitlán to the ground. He built a new city on top of the ruins. This city was called "Mexico City." It became the capital of **New Spain** (see p. 67) and the greatest city in the Spanish American Empire.

De Soto, Hernando (ca. 1498–1542)

Spanish explorer and slave trader. Hernando de Soto was only sixteen when he joined an *expedition* to the West Indies. In 1523, he joined Francisco Fernandez de Córdoba on an expedition to Nicaragua. He helped explore and colonize Nicaragua. While he lived there, he became wealthy in the slave trade. In 1532, de Soto went with **Francisco Pizarro** (see p. 68) on his expedition to conquer the **Inca** (see p. 27) peoples.

In 1536, De Soto returned to **Spain** (see p. 39). By 1539, he had sailed once more for the *New World*. De Soto landed on the west coast of **Florida** (see p. 58). He arrived with ten ships and a thousand armed men. Over the next four years, they searched for silver and gold. They explored parts of present-day Florida, South Carolina, North Carolina, Alabama, Mississippi, Tennessee, Arkansas, Oklahoma, and **Texas** (see p. 91). De Soto badly mistreated the Native Americans he encountered. He and his expedition survived because of their vast supply of weapons and numerous soldiers. De Soto and his expedition discovered the Mississippi River in 1541. Hernando de Soto died of fever while on this expedition.

encomendero

Privileged colonist who received "tribute" from conquered peoples. The Spanish explorers came to the Americas looking for wealth and fame. When Native American peoples were conquered, the Spanish expected them to pay tribute, a kind of tax. They forced the Native Americans to give them large portions of their harvests or other goods. The tribute was called encomienda (*en-coh-me-EHN-duh*). Only a few explorers or settlers were allowed to claim encomienda. These people were the *encomenderos* (*en-coh-men-ehn-DARE-ohs*). The Spanish king gave the *encomenderos* permission to demand food, animal hides, and blankets from the Native Americans. In return for these goods, the *encomenderos* promised military service to the Spanish king. They also were supposed to protect the Spanish colony and convert Native Americans to Christianity. The encomenderos took a great deal from the conquered peoples and became very wealthy.

Estéban (ca. 1500–1539)

Enslaved man and explorer. Estéban was born in Azamor, Morocco. He was with **Álvar Núñez Cabeza de Vaca** (see p. 51) on the ill-fated voyage to **Florida** (see p. 58). Estéban was one of the four remaining members of the *expedition* who arrived on the Gulf coast of **Texas** (see p. 91). The four men traveled through Texas and northern **Mexico** (see p. 62). The group encountered many Native Americans. Estéban would speak with them and offer to heal their sick. He became known as a man of peace. This reputation kept the four men safe on their three-year journey. Estéban, Cabeza de Vaca, and the others reached Mexico City in 1536. In 1539, the viceroy, or royal governor, of Mexico, Antonio de Mendoza (*an-TO-nee-oh duh men-DOH-zuh*), chose Estéban to guide the Franciscan *monk* Father Marcos de Niza on an expedition to what is now the southwestern United States. Father de Niza was unable to complete the journey. He sent Estéban on to continue the exploration. After a while, Estéban disappeared. It is believed that the Native American Zuñi killed him in about 1539.

Florida

Peninsula located in the southeast corner of North America. **Juan Ponce de León** (see p. 69) discovered Florida in 1513. It wasn't until 1521 that he tried to establish a colony there. The native peoples in the area resisted, and Ponce de León was killed. Over the next thirty years, other Spanish explorers visited the shores and interior of Florida. In 1528, **Pánfilo de Narváez** (see p. 65) explored the interior of what is now Georgia. The search for gold and other treasure brought **Hernando de Soto** (see p. 56) to Florida. He did not find gold, but he did find the Mississippi River. Florida was proving to be difficult for the Spanish explorers to settle. Other explorers started to lose interest in Florida.

Twenty years after De Soto's *expedition*, **Spain** (see p. 39) once again became interested in Florida. At this time, there were other European nations beginning to explore parts of the North American continent. Spain wanted to protect its interests. Florida was located in a good spot to do this. Spain also had many ships sailing back to the Old World. These ships carried treasure that other European countries wanted. Spanish colonies in Florida could help protect these ships.

In 1565, Pedro Menéndez de Avilés founded the city of St. Augustine. He did this by destroying a French settlement that was already there. He killed all of the people who lived in the settlement. By the seventeenth century, Spain had established many

Juana Inés de la Cruz

(Library of Congress)

A seventeenth-century Roman Catholic nun, scholar, and poet, Sister Juana (*WHA-nuh*) Inés de la Cruz was born near Mexico City. By age four, she could read and write, and she mastered Latin after only twenty lessons. At nineteen years old, she became a Catholic nun. While in the convent, Sister Juana pursued her lifelong love of learning. She could speak intelligently on many subjects, from philosophy and the arts to history and astronomy. She also wrote numerous books of poetry, plays, and scholarly essays. Sister Juana was one of the first to fight for the equality of women, especially the right of women to be educated. Sister Juana Inés de la Cruz died in 1694 of the plague (*PLAYG*).

missions (see p. 64) in Florida. Pensacola, on the Florida panhandle, was founded in 1698. While Spain was establishing colonies in Florida, the English and French were doing the same farther north. By 1682, England and France had settlements bordering the Spanish colonies in Florida. This weakened Spain's hold on Florida. By the mid-eighteenth century, enemy territory surrounded Spanish Florida.

Kino, Father Eusebio Francisco (1645-1711)

Jesuit *missionary* and explorer. Father Eusebio Francisco Kino was born in Italy and was educated in Germany. He learned astronomy, mathematics, and mapmaking. In 1665, he entered the priesthood. In 1681, he sailed from **Spain** (see p. 39) to Mexico City to become a missionary. Father Kino wanted to teach the Roman Catholic faith to the native peoples in the *New World*. In 1691, he began the first of over forty *expeditions* to the area. He explored the territories of present-day northern **Mexico** (see p. 63), southern **California** (see p. 104), and southern Arizona. He also explored along the Rio Grande, Colorado, and Gila Rivers. Father Kino was the first to map that part of North America.

Father Kino founded many **missions** (see p. 64) among the Yaqui (*yah-KEE*), Yuma (*YOO-muh*), and **Akimel O'odham** (*ah-KEE-mel OH-uhd-uhm*) (see p. 19) peoples. He introduced the first horses and cattle to the Pima. He brought them new kinds of seeds. He also taught them new ways to farm. At the time, many Native Americans in the Spanish colonies were forced to work in silver mines. Father Kino fought to stop this forced labor. He died in Mexico in 1711.

Las Casas, Bartolomé de (1474–1566)

Bartolomé de Las Casas
(Library of Congress)

Historian, missionary, advocate for Native Americans. Bartolomé de Las Casas (*bart-TAHL-oh-may duh las CAS-us*) began his adult career as a soldier. In 1502, he traveled to Hispaniola. He took part in some explorations and was rewarded. He was given an encomienda. (See **encomendero** [see p. 57].) Over the next twelve years, Las Casas witnessed the suffering of the Native American peoples. He decided to become a priest. In 1512 or 1513, Las Casas became the first man to be ordained a priest in the *New World*. As a priest, he was part of the bloody conquest of Cuba in 1513. His experiences during the conquest taught him even more about the injustices the Native Americans were forced to endure.

Las Casas felt he could better help the Native Americans by returning to **Spain** (see p. 39). In 1515, he spoke of the Native Americans to church officials. A plan of reform was created. In 1516, Las Casas sailed once again for the Americas. He fought to find ways for the Spanish colonists and Native Americans to live together peacefully. He did not have much success. The Spanish colonists continued to badly mistreat the Native Americans.

Las Casas wrote a history of the Spanish treatment of the Native Americans. It was called *Historia de Las Indias*. In it, he gives much detail about the horrible suffering the Native Americans endured at the hands of the Spanish conquerors. The information from that book and other writings of Las Casas led to reform of some laws in the Spanish colonies. These laws were called the "New Laws." The *encomienda* system (see **encomendero**, p. 57) changed under the New Laws. Mistreatment of Native Americans was forbidden. Despite the law, however, these things did not change very much.

The Suffering of the Native Americans

Bartolomé de Las Casas (1474–1566) was a missionary who witnessed the harsh mistreatment of Native Americans by Spanish soldiers. He became a tireless fighter to stop this mistreatment. He journeyed to Spain and persuaded the Spanish king to create the New Laws in 1642. These laws should have protected the Native Americans from the abuses they suffered at the hands of the Spanish soldiers. Unfortunately, they were rarely enforced. In his writings, Las Casas described what he had seen. This excerpt is from his book written in 1542, *Brief Report on the Destruction of the Indians.*

One time the Indians came to meet us, and to receive us with **victuals**, and delicate cheere, and with all entertainment ten leagues off a great Citie, and being come at the place, they presented us with a great quantity of fish, and of bread, and other meate, together with all that they could doe for us to the uttermost. See incontinent **the Divell**, which put himselfe into the Spaniards, to **put them all to the edge of the sword** in my presence, without any cause whatsoever, more than three thousand soules, which were set before us, men, women, and children. I saw there so great cruelties that never any many living either have or shall see the like.

◀ **victuals**
food

◀ **the Divell**
the Devil

◀ **put them all to the edge of the sword**
killed them with swords

Las Casas worked hard to improve the lives of the Native Americans in the Spanish colonies up to his death at age ninety-two. Many of Bartolomé de Las Casas's writings influenced later heroes of Mexican independence.

Louisiana Territory

Area in southeastern North America. The explorations of **Juan Ponce de León** (see p. 69) in **Florida** (see p. 58) and **Hernando de Soto** (see p. 56) in the southeast established the Spanish presence in that area of North America. De Soto's explorations of the Mississippi River territory pushed Spanish land claims even farther. Based on these explorations, **Spain** (see p. 39) claimed vast amounts of land on both sides of the Mississippi River.

In 1682, French explorers from Quebec in Canada challenged those claims. The French said that all the lands around the Mississippi belonged to France. Soon, the French were attacking parts of Spanish-held Florida. They then crossed the Mississippi and claimed territory in what are now Kansas, Oklahoma, and **Texas** (see p. 91). The Spanish believed these lands were theirs. The fighting between the two countries over these territories ended in 1763. France gave to Spain all of the land west of the Mississippi to the Rocky Mountains. This territory included everything from the Gulf of Mexico in the south to the border of Canada in the north. This area became known as "**Louisiana**" (see p. 83). Spain held this territory until the American colonists started to slowly take pieces of Louisiana away from the Spanish in the nineteenth century.

mestizo

People of mixed white and Native American ancestry. By the beginning of the eighteenth century, most of the people living in Hispanic America were part–Native American peoples, or *mestizo* (*mes-TEES-oh*). The mestizo had both white and Native American ancestors. Many of the Spanish and other European settlers had intermarried with Native Americans. The mestizo were the result of these unions. In the early 1800s, there were over five million people of mixed ancestry in the Spanish colonies. Most of these were mestizo. The numbers of mestizo continued to grow along with the settlements of **New Spain** (see p. 67). These peoples laid the cultural foundation of today's Hispanic America.

Mexico

For thousands of years, Mexico had been the home of some of the most advanced peoples in the world. The **Olmec** (see p. 33), Toltec, and **Maya** (see p. 29) peoples who lived there built pyramids and studied *astronomy* and other sciences. They developed systems of writing and record keeping. These peoples had achieved these things long before the people in Europe were able to do so. By the fifteenth century, Mexico already had a long history of civilization.

Human Sacrifice among the Aztec

José de Acosta (1539–1600) was a Jesuit missionary in Peru and Mexico. His book, ***The Natural and Moral History of the Indies***, is the earliest survey of the New World and how it compares to the Old World. In this excerpt, de Acosta describes the ritual the Aztec used in their human sacrifices to the Aztec gods.

In truth, the Mexicans did not sacrifice any to their idols but Captives, and the ordinary **warres** they made, was onely to have Captives for their Sacrifices. . . . The manner they used in their Sacrifices, was, they assembled within the Palissadoe of dead mens Sculles such as should be sacrificed, using a certayne Ceremony at the foot of the Palissadoe, placing a great guard about them. Presently, there stept forth a Priest, attyred with a short Surplice full of tassels beneath, who came from the top of the Temple with an Idoll made of Paste of Wheate and **Mays** mingled with Honey, which had the eyes made of the graines of greene glasse, and the teeth the graines of Mays, he descended the steps of the Temple with all speed he could, and mounted on a great stone planted upon a high Terrasse in the midst of the Court . . . . The ordinary manner of sacrificing was, to open the stomake of him that was sacrificed, and having pulled out his heart halfe alive, they tumbled the man downe the staires of the Temple, which were all imbrewed and defiled with bloud.

◀ **warres**
wars

◀ **Mays**
maize, or corn

By the end of the fifteenth century, the land now known as Mexico was part of the huge **Aztec** (see p. 20) Empire. These peoples were also an advanced civilization. They were descended from the ancient Olmec and Toltec peoples. In 1519, the Spanish explorer, **Hernán Cortés** (see p. 55) began his conquest of the Aztec. After many battles, he defeated the Aztec in 1521 and claimed all of their empire for Spain.

Cortés's conquest of Mexico created the anchor for the new Spanish Empire in the Americas. Mexico became the heart of Spanish America. There, explorers and colonists first blended the Spanish and Native American traditions. Many explorations into the southwestern part of North America originated from Mexico. The first and most powerful government in Spanish America was also located in Mexico as well. Mexico was the key to all of Spanish America throughout the three hundred years of Spanish rule.

missions

Religious settlements. The **conquistadors** (see p. 54) and explorers came to the Americas in search of wealth. Spreading their Christian faith was usually just as important. Many expeditions traveling to unknown lands included priests as well as soldiers. The priests went along to meet the spiritual needs of the soldiers. They were present also to convert Native Americans to Christianity. To do this, the Spanish established missions in the territories the soldiers conquered. Sometimes missions were built before any military action took place. The Spanish used the missions to make the first important contact with the Native American peoples in the area.

The missions were governed by Spanish priests called missionaries. Sometimes, the missionaries were almost as cruel to the Native Americans as were the conquistadors. They forced the Native Americans to build mission houses and churches. They forced them to work in the fields to grow crops for the mission. More often, however, the missionaries tried to make sure that the Native Americans were treated fairly. Many missionaries learned the language of the Native Americans to better communicate with them. **Bartolomé de Las Casas** (*bart-TAHL-oh-may duh las CAS-us*) (see p. 60) was one missionary who treated Native Americans with kindness.

The missions provided a means of blending some of the Spanish traditions with those of the Native Americans. Music, played during religious services, might include instruments from both cultures. The mission schools taught the Spanish language to the native peoples. Mission hospitals helped the sick of both cultures. The presence of the missions and the priests helped Native Americans better understand some of the Spanish who were quickly moving into native lands.

Narváez, Pánfilo de (ca. 1478-1528)

Spanish **conquistador** (see p. 54) and explorer. Pánfilo de

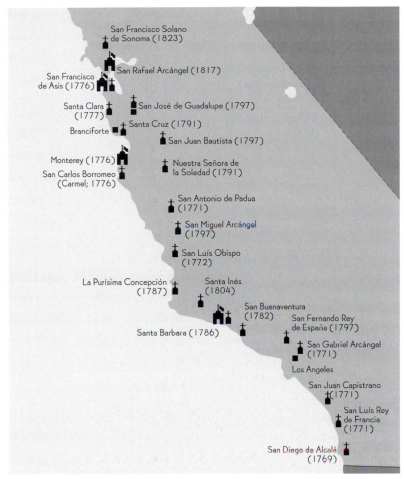

San Francisco Solano
† de Sonoma (1823)

San Rafael Arcángel (1817)

San Francisco
de Asis (1776)

Santa Clara †
(1777)   † San José de Guadalupe (1797)

Branciforte   † Santa Cruz (1791)

† San Juan Bautista (1797)

Monterey (1776)

San Carlos Borromeo   † Nuestra Señora de
(Carmel; 1776)   la Soledad (1791)

† San Antonio de Padua
  (1771)

† San Miguel Arcángel
  (1797)

† San Luís Obispo
  (1772)

La Purísima Concepción   Santa Inés
(1787)   (1804)

San Buenaventura
(1782)

San Fernando Rey
de España (1797)

Santa Barbara (1786)

† San Gabriel Arcángel
  (1771)

Los Angeles

San Juan Capistrano
†(1771)

San Luís Rey
de Francia
(1771)

San Diego de Alcalá †
(1769)

Father Juniperro Serra helped found religious missions throughout California in the late eighteenth century.

Narváez (*pahn-FEE-oh duh nar-VAY-ez*) became a soldier as a young man. He was one of the first settlers on the Caribbean island of Jamaica. In 1511, Narváez commanded a group of archers during the conquest of Cuba. He was given many honors and land in Cuba as rewards for his service. In 1520, he sailed from Cuba bound for **Mexico** (see p. 62) with a large number of ships. Narváez had been ordered by the king of **Spain** (see p. 39) to capture and replace **Hernán Cortés** (see p. 55) as ruler of Mexico. Instead, Cortés defeated Narváez and imprisoned him and his crew.

Narváez was released in 1521 and returned to Cuba. In 1527, the Spanish king gave him permission to lead an *expedition* to colonize **Florida** (see p. 58). Narváez left Spain with five ships and about six hundred sailors, soldiers, and colonists. In Cuba, a hurricane sank two of the ships. The expedition did not reach the west coast of Florida until 1528. **Álvar Núñez Cabeza de Vaca** (see p. 51) was with him on this expedition. Narváez and his expedition were stranded in Florida. While his expedition was on land, the crew took the ships and deserted the explorers. Narváez and his men in the expedition tried to sail to Mexico on rafts. They managed to sail along the northern Gulf of Mexico. They passed the mouth of the Mississippi River. Narváez never completed his journey to Mexico. Storms blew his raft out to sea, and he was lost.

New Mexico

Area in southwestern North America. Between 1528 and 1536, **Álvar Núñez Cabeza de Vaca** (see p. 51) walked through parts of what would come to be called New Mexico on his way to Mexico City. His stories of the Seven Cities of Cíbola led **Francisco Coronado** (see p. 54) also to explore part of this territory in 1540. Both explorers reported that there were not many people living in this territory. Nor did they report finding any riches. **Spain** (see p. 39) did not pursue more exploration until the late sixteenth century. Explorations by other European nations caused the government in **New Spain** (see p. 67) to worry about its northern borders. New Spain did not want the lands just north of **Mexico** (see p. 62) to be claimed by another nation.

In 1598, Juan de Oñate left Mexico with an *expedition* to the area the Spanish called *Nueva Mexico*, "New Mexico." De Oñate founded the town of San Juan de los Caballeros near what is now Santa Fe. His cruel treatment of the Native Americans in New Mexico led to the **Pueblo Revolt** (see p. 70) in 1680. The Spanish recaptured the area from the Native Americans in 1696. Soon, **missions** (see p. 64) were built in New Mexico and in the area that would come to be called Arizona.

By 1800, most of the people living in New Mexico were **mestizo** (see p. 62). The mestizo blended the heritages of the Spanish and Native American peoples. Later in the nineteenth century, New Mexico became an important center for trade with Arizona, **California** (see p. 104), and **Texas** (see p. 91). A very well-used trade route, El Camino Real, passed through New Mexico.

New Spain

A territory in New Spain governed by representatives of the king of **Spain** (see p. 39). By 1535, Spain had colonized large areas of North and South America. The Spanish king decided that it was very difficult to govern all of this territory from Spain. He divided the land claimed by Spain into smaller territories. These were called "viceroyalties" (*vice-ROY-uhl-tees*).

One of these territories was the viceroyalty of New Spain. This area included all Spanish-held land north of what is now the *Isthmus* of Panama. New Spain included all of **Mexico** (see p. 62), **California** (see p. 104), the southern part of North America all the way to **Florida** (see p. 58), and the Caribbean Islands. In 1565, the Pacific islands now known as the Philippines were added to New Spain.

A viceroy governed each viceroyalty. The viceroy was appointed by the king of Spain to act in the king's name. The viceroy was

This map shows what New Spain looked like in 1600. It included Mexico, Florida, most of Central America, the Caribbean Islands, and part of South America.

Privateers and Pirates

As the New World was being settled, different countries battled over claims on territory. These disagreements led to rival countries attacking one another's ships at sea. The English and the Spanish were old enemies, competing for territory in the New World. England paid skilled sailors, called privateers, to attack and rob Spanish ships returning to Spain with gold and goods from the New World. Privateers also attacked cities located on the coasts. Sir Francis Drake and Sir John Hawkins were two infamous English privateers. Both tried to attack Spanish-held Puerto Rico.

By the end of the sixteenth century, pirates had replaced privateers. Unlike the privateers, pirates did not work for a particular government. They robbed ships for their own profit. Pirates attacked any ship that carried something the pirates wanted—usually gold or the possessions of the ships' passengers. They also terrorized many port cities. Pirates such as Edward Teach, known as Blackbeard, made their bases on the Caribbean islands of Tortuga and Jamaica. They would sail from these ports to attack ships at sea.

responsible for converting the Native Americans to Christianity, building schools, and managing the economy. The first viceroy of New Spain was Antonio de Mendoza, who ruled from 1535 to 1549. During his rule, he sent **Francisco Vásquez de Coronado** (see p. 54) to explore much of the southwestern part of North America. He also tried to help the Native American peoples who had suffered at the hands of the **conquistadors** (see p. 54).

Pizarro, Francisco (ca. 1475–1541)

Spanish explorer, conqueror of Peru. Francisco Pizarro came to the *New World* in 1510 seeking fame and fortune. He was with **Vasco Núñez de Balboa** (see p. 51) on his journey across Central America. Pizarro hoped to follow in the footsteps of **Hernán Cortés** (see p. 55). He wanted to gain glory by conquering an empire, as Cortés had done. Pizzaro had heard from some of the native peoples about the **Inca** (see p. 27). The Inca were from a rich city in what is now Peru. He received permission from the king of **Spain** (see p. 39) to find and conquer the Inca nation. In 1531, Pizarro sailed from Panama. He reached Peru in 1532.

By 1535, many Inca had died from smallpox that had been introduced into the area by Spanish explorers. The Incan king was one of those who died. Two of his sons fought each other for control of the Inca Empire. Their disagreement made it easier for Pizarro to attack. One of the brothers had just defeated the other when Pizarro arrived. He was accompanied by **Hernando de Soto** (see p. 56). Pizarro and his army invaded the cities of the Inca in 1532. He used many of the same methods **Cortés** (see p. 55) had used to defeat the **Aztec** (see p. 20) in **Mexico** (see p. 63). Pizarro terrified the Inca with firearms and steel swords. Even the horses Pizarro and his men rode added to the Inca's fear. He tricked, trapped, and murdered the new emperor and took over the capital city of Cuzco. In 1535, Pizarro realized that Cuzco was located too far from the coast to be an effective capital. He founded a new city near the coast and named it Ciudad de los Reyes, "City of the Kings." The city became Lima, the capital of Peru. In 1541, Pizarro was assassinated during a civil war in Peru.

Ponce de León, Juan (1460–1521)

Spanish explorer. In 1493, Juan Ponce de León (*wahn PAHNS duh lay-OWN*) joined **Christopher Columbus** (see p. 52) on Columbus's second trip to Hispaniola. In 1508, he led the successful *expedition* to conquer Puerto Rico. He was named Puerto Rico's governor. Puerto Rico had many gold mines. The Native American peoples there were forced to work in those mines. Ponce de León became one of the richest men in the Caribbean. In 1513, he went in search of more gold and more Native Americans to enslave. He sailed northwest from Puerto Rico. He landed on the Atlantic coast of **Florida** (see p. 58). Ponce de León believed he had found an island and claimed it for **Spain** (see p. 39). He called it "Florida" because he had found it during the Easter season. In Spanish, that season is called Pascua Florida. Ponce de León did not stay in Florida. He returned to Puerto Rico with plans to return to Florida. He made a second voyage in 1521. This time, he wanted to establish a colony. The Native Americans who lived there were the Calusa (*cal-OOS-uh*). They resisted the expedition's attempts to build a settlement. During the battle, Ponce de León was wounded. He died in Cuba of those wounds.

Juan Ponce de León
(Library of Congress)

Pueblo Revolt

Native American rebellion. In 1598, Spanish explorer Juan de Oñate (*oh-NYA-tay*), founded a settlement in the **New Mexico** (see p. 66) territory. He named the settlement San Juan de los Caballeros (*san WAHN duh los cab-ay-AIR-os*). This was close to present-day Santa Fe, New Mexico. Oñate became the governor of this settlement. He badly mistreated the local Native Americans. Because of this, he was replaced in 1607 with a new governor—Pedro de Peralta. In 1610, Peralta founded the town of Santa Fe. The Spanish forced the **Pueblo** (*PWEB-lo*) (see p. 36) peoples to build the mission and town buildings. The Spanish abused and murdered them. In 1680, the Pueblo peoples revolted.

A Tewa (*TEE-wah*) named Popé led the revolt. Popé was a shaman (*SHAH-muhn*), a holy man or priest. He gathered the Hopi, Zuñi, and Acoma peoples, who were all members of the Pueblo nation. These peoples wanted to practice the religion of their ancestors. They destroyed the Spanish missions. They killed four hundred Spanish and forced the rest to leave. The Pueblo peoples controlled Santa Fe for more than ten years. In 1692, the Spanish returned. They recaptured Santa Fe. By 1696, they had also recaptured the surrounding territory.

The Spanish then treated the Pueblo a little better. They allowed the Pueblo to perform their traditional ceremonies. In later years, the Apache peoples started to raid both the Pueblo and Spanish settlements. The Pueblo joined with the Spanish colonists to defend themselves against the Apache.

Serra, Junípero (1713-1784)

Spanish priest and missionary. Father Junípero Serra (*hoo-nee-PARE-oh SARE-uh*) was born in Spain and became a Franciscan priest at the age of eighteen. In 1750, he traveled as a missionary in **Mexico** (see p. 62) *converting* Native Americans. He founded **missions** (see p. 64) there and lived in Mexico until 1767. Father Serra then traveled north from Mexico into southern **California** (see p. 104) to continue his mission work. He founded his first mission in California at San Diego. Father Serra encouraged poor Spanish settlers to move to the mission. He wanted them to build homes and farms and to use local Native Americans as laborers.

Few Native Americans were willing to stay on the missions unless they were forced. Nor did they understand farming, since they lived by hunting and fishing. Nonetheless, Father Serra stuck with his goal of converting all Native Americans with whom he came in contact. Slowly, towns grew around the missions. Father Serra founded many missions along the California coast. Towns grew around some of those missions, as they had in San Diego. These towns include Los Angeles, San Francisco, Santa Clara, and Carmel.

Spanish America, economy of

The economy of Spanish America rested on the backs of Native Americans and enslaved Africans. Wealth in the colonies was held in the hands of a few people. These people were landowners, merchants, and factory and mine owners. To make the most money possible, the wealthy depended on the free or almost free labor of the Native American peoples and enslaved Africans. There was a system of forced labor called *repartimiento*, which provided owners of large estates with workers. Enslaved Africans were also purchased to work the land and in the mines.

Gold and silver were the most valuable exports from the colonies. Honduras, Guatemala, **Mexico** (see p. 62), and Bolivia were the sources for these precious metals. Spanish America also exported many agricultural products. Tobacco, sugar, and cacao were three important exports sent back to the Old World. Spanish America also imported goods. Colonists bought iron, wine, cloth, olive oil, furniture, books, and slaves. Spain controlled the trade from Spanish America. Goods from the *New World* could go only to Spain or to other territories held by Spain.

Spanish Armada

Spanish fleet. In the late 1500s, English *privateers* attacked Spanish ships and port cities in the *New World*. King Philip II of **Spain** (see p. 39) wanted to stop the attacks. He assembled a mighty fleet of 125 warships known as the Spanish Armada. King Philip sent the Armada to defeat the British navy and to invade England. In 1588, the Armada approached the eastern shore of England. Sir Francis Drake commanded an English fleet against the Armada. The battle between the two navies lasted twelve hours. Although the Armada was much larger than the English force, the Spanish were defeated. The destruction of the Spanish Armada hurt Spain's ability to protect its New World colonies from attack by sea. The English continued to attack Spanish ships returning to Spain from the New World.

Treaty of Tordesillas (1494)

Agreement about newly discovered lands. In 1493, **King Ferdinand II of Aragon and Queen Isabella I of Castile** (see p. 25), the rulers of **Spain**, (see p. 39), had received the reports of **Christopher Columbus**'s (see p. 52) discoveries in the *New World*. Portugal was Spain's main competitor in exploring new lands. The Spanish wanted to be sure that all the lands in the New World would belong to them. They asked the Spanish-born Pope Alexander VI to help them. He created a boundary line that ran from the North Pole to the South Pole. The pope declared that all lands west of this boundary would belong to Spain. These lands included territories that had not yet been discovered.

Portugal disagreed with the pope's decision. Its explorers had been the first to sail down the coast of Africa. According to the pope's orders, Portugal could not sail to the ports it had already established there. The Portuguese also wanted to claim new lands in the Americas. In 1494, Spanish and Portuguese ambassadors met to reach an agreement. This agreement was called the Treaty of Tordesillas (*tor-duh-SEE-us*). In this treaty, a new boundary line was chosen. This boundary allowed Portugal to claim the coast of Brazil. The Portuguese explorer Pedro Alvares Cabral had discovered this part of the New World in 1500. This also allowed Portugal to expand its explorations into South America.

CHAPTER THREE

La Independencia

Independence in Hispanic America, 1776–1823

"[Creoles] are frequently heard to declare with pride, 'I am not a Spaniard, I am an American,' words which reveal the symptoms of a long resentment."

—Alexander von Humboldt, 1811

By the end of the eighteenth century, **Spain** (see p. 39) had controlled most of the territory in the New World for more than 250 years. During this time, thousands of Spanish immigrants arrived. They brought along their Spanish traditions and beliefs. The native peoples the Spanish had conquered greeted them. These peoples had their own traditions and beliefs. Living side by side for hundreds of years, both groups changed. The culture of the conquerors blended with the culture of the people they had conquered.

Throughout the Americas, new peoples emerged. Some were criollos (*CREE-yo-los*), or Creoles (*cree-YOL-z*), people of Spanish descent born in the Americas. Some were **mestizos** (*mes-TEE-sohs*) (see p. 62), people who have both Spanish and Native American ancestors. Still others were mulattoes (*moo-LAHT-ohs*), people of both African and European heritage. In Spanish America, these new people brought new ideas.

Many colonists in the Americas no longer felt the strong ties to Spain. These Spanish Americans began to adopt a sense of belonging to the region where they lived. They felt that their roots were in the Americas, not in distant Spain. Although they spoke Spanish, they did not feel themselves to be the same type of people who lived in Spain. Most Creoles, mestizos, and mulattoes saw themselves as Spanish Americans. They recognized their Spanish heritage. But they also identified with the heritage of their ancestors in the Americas.

The Spanish Americans in all the colonies began to resent Spanish rule. They felt many laws were unfair. For example, Spain limited the number of places where Spanish Americans could sell their goods. This arrangement made the sale of the goods more profitable for Spain. However, it did not at all benefit the Spanish Americans. Taxes were also a point of disagreement. The taxes the Spanish Americans paid seemed to benefit only Spain. They saw that their hard work created wealth for people in a country they had never seen. Spain seemed very far away.

There were even serious problems with the government officials sent by Spain to govern the colonies. They were supposed to protect the Spanish Americans. Many times, this did not happen. The government officials were often dishonest and corrupt. The Spanish Americans saw that the highest government posts were given only to people who had been born in Spain, not to people who represented the largest populations. The American-born colonists were uncomfortable under Spain's rule. Some wondered whether the time for Spanish control had passed. They began to consider changing their situation. Events in Europe fired their imaginations about what might be possible in Spanish America.

In Europe, the lower classes were challenging ways of thinking that had been in place for centuries. The French Revolution in 1789 limited the power of kings. A government formed by common people replaced the old method of rule. The armies of this new government won battle after battle

Timeline

1779

Spain declares war on England during the **American Revolution**.

1783

By signing the Treaty of Paris, Great Britain not only grants the United States its independence, but also gives **East and West Florida** to Spain.

against very powerful enemies. The French seemed to have successfully created a new form of government.

The **American Revolution** (see p. 79) in 1776 had shown Spanish America that colonies could successfully throw off the control of the "mother" country. Again, the common people had overthrown the rule of kings. Spanish Americans began to see that they, too, could win their independence.

The Spanish Americans needed only one more spark to fire their dreams of independence. They needed some point around which they could unite. The spark came from an unlikely source. It came from the actions of a French general.

In 1808, General Napoléon Bonaparte (*nap-PO-lee-on BO-nuh-part*) tried to make his brother the king of Spain. The Spanish rejected Napoléon's brother. In 1812, they revolted. The people of Spanish America also united against Napoléon's actions. Many European Spanish and Spanish Americans wanted King Ferdinand VII to resume the throne. They supported the return of the Spanish king because they were not quite ready for real independence from Spain. However, both the European and American Spanish wanted Ferdinand back only under certain conditions. In 1812, the people of Spain had created the Constitution of Cádiz (*cah-DEEZ*). This constitution placed specific limits on the king's power. When Ferdinand VII returned to the Spanish throne in 1814, he overturned this constitution. He declared that he

1789	**1793**	**1795**	**1796**
Beginning of the French Revolution. Four years later Austria, Prussia, the Netherlands, Spain, and Great Britain join forces to fight the new French Republic.	Treaty of Paris gives **East and West Florida** to Spain.	The victorious French government forces Spain to give up its colony of Santo Domingo.	Spain forms an alliance with France against England. This begins Napoléon's control of the Spanish throne.

would take back all the powers previously awarded to the king. His action surprised many in Spain. It also gave momentum to the independence movements brewing in Spanish America.

In 1810, some people took the first actions toward independence in **Mexico** (see p. 62). Father Miguel Hidalgo y Costilla (*mee-GEL hee-dahl-go ee cos-TEE-yuh*) gathered Native Americans, **mestizos** (see p. 62), and other poor members of his parish. Father Hidalgo wanted to abolish slavery and help the mestizo and Native American peoples rise out of poverty. He led them in revolt against the Spanish government. Although he was soon defeated, Hidalgo had started the Spanish Americans in Mexico on the path to true independence. Other Spanish Americans in Mexico, such as José María Morelos y Pavón (*ho-SAY muh-REE-uh mor-AY-os ee pah-VON*) and Vincente Guerrero (*vin-SENT-ay ger-RARE-oh*), continued the fight. By 1821, Mexico had won independence from Spain (see **Mexican War of Independence**, p. 84). The Central American states located between and including Guatemala and Costa Rica followed Mexico's lead and declared their independence (see **Central American wars of independence**, p. 80).

In South America, Francisco de Miranda (*fran-SEES-coh duh mir-AHN-duh*) was a strong force for independence. As early as 1806, he had led a revolution in Venezuela and became dictator. The revolution was brief. Miranda was overthrown, but he inspired an even greater South American leader. Simón Bolívar took up the cause of independence from Miranda. From 1811 until

1799	**1803**	**1804**	**1810**
Napoléon Bonaparte takes control of the armies of the French Republic. He names himself dictator of France. The Napoleonic Wars begin. A year later, he forces King Charles IV of Spain to give **Louisiana** back to France.	Napoléon sells **Louisiana** to the United States for $15 million.	Napoléon persuades Spain to declare war on Great Britain. A year later, he places his brother Joseph Bonaparte on the Spanish throne.	Father Miguel Hidalgo y Costilla begins the **Mexican War of Independence** with the "Grito de Dolores."

1819, Bolívar led many battles in Venezuela and Colombia against forces loyal to Spain. In 1819, he achieved success in an important battle in New Granada, present-day Colombia. This allowed Colombia, Venezuela, and Panama to unite under the name "Gran Colombia." By 1824, Venezuela, Colombia, and Ecuador had all won independence from Spain (see **South American wars of independence**, p. 90).

José de San Martín also led important revolutions in South America. While Bolívar swept down from the north, San Martín moved up from the south. Between 1811 and 1826, San Martín helped Uruguay, Paraguay, Argentina, Chile, and Bolivia become free of Spain's control.

In the Caribbean, an uprising, led by a formerly enslaved African named François-Dominique Toussaint-Louverture (*fran-SWAH doh-min-EEK too-SAHNT low-vuh-CHURE*), freed the Spanish colony of Santo Domingo. This had been Spain's first colony in the New World. By 1821, Santo Domingo had won its independence. (See **Caribbean colonies wars of independence**, p. 80).

By 1826, all of Spain's colonies except Cuba and Puerto Rico had claimed independence. Each of these colonies then became a separate country or state. Each reflected unique regional influences. For example, the people who lived in Mexico developed a distinct Mexican tradition. The people in Peru developed *cultural* characteristics that can be found nowhere else. Unique blends of Spanish and local cultures characterized the newly independent regions.

1812	**1817**	**1818**	**1819**
War begins between the United States and England.	First **Seminole War** begins.	Chile declares its independence from Spain. Venezuela will follow in 1820, Ecuador and Central America in 1822, and Peru in 1824.	Spain signs the Adams-Onís Treaty giving **Florida** to the United States.
The Duke of Wellington moves against Napoléon in Spain. He defeats Napoléon the following year.	American general Andrew Jackson invades Spanish **Florida**.		

Each region created its own approach to food, clothing, and religious ceremonies. Each created its own identity and history. Yet they all shared one important cultural characteristic. The people of these newly independent countries spoke Spanish. Their common language linked all Spanish Americans. This link remains today for the descendents of those people who first claimed independence from Spain. Today's Spanish Americans, or Hispanic Americans, have their roots in many countries with many traditions.

1821	1822	1822
Spain signs the Treaty of Córdoba that grants independence to Mexico.	Augustín de Iturbide declares himself Augustín I, Emperor of Mexico.	Augustín I is overthrown by Mexican revolutionaries.

A-Z of Key People, Places and Terms

American Revolution (1775-1783)

War fought by the American colonies in North America to obtain independence from Great Britain. During the seventeenth and eighteenth centuries, England was one of **Spain**'s (see p. 39) chief competitors for territory in the *New World*. Spain held much more land, but English territories often bordered Spain's. English pirates and *privateers* had captured many of Spain's ships traveling to Europe from the New World. These activities had cost Spain a great deal of money. By the late eighteenth century, Spain was very interested in doing whatever it could to break England's power.

England claimed territory in North America known as the Thirteen Colonies. In 1776, representatives of these colonies declared independence from Great Britain. Spain and France both saw a chance to push Great Britain out of North America. These two countries believed that if Great Britain lost its territories, Spain and France could increase theirs. They decided to help the American colonists in the war against England.

Spain and France gave the colonists weapons, food, and money. They allowed the colonists' ships to use their ports to load and unload necessary goods. The Spanish governor of Louisiana, Bernardo de Gálvez (*ber-NARD-oh duh gal-VEZ*), protected the colonists' ships by fooling the English. He pretended to capture the ships. When the English ships left, de Gálvez released the colonists' ships. He also allowed cattle from the Spanish territory that is now **Texas** (see p. 91) to be driven across **Louisiana** (see p. 83). This provided food for the colonial armies.

Spain and France also helped the armies of the American Revolution by attacking Great Britain in 1779. This forced the British to divide their powerful navy. They sent some ships to fight the colonists. Others were kept behind to defend Great Britain from the French and Spanish navies. Because of this, the British army in North American could not get the help it needed to defeat the colonists. In 1781, the English surrendered.

For their help during the American Revolution, Spain gained the territories of **East and West Florida** (See p. 82). Spain had succeeded in helping to drive England from North America. However, Spain soon found that the success of the American Revolution led to unrest in its colonies.

Caribbean colonies wars of independence

Wars in the Spanish-held Caribbean colonies. Puerto Rico, Cuba, and **Santo Domingo** (see p. 89) were the most important colonies held by **Spain** (see p. 39) near the end of the eighteenth century. The wars for independence from Spain only succeeded in Santo Domingo. In 1821, François-Dominique Toussaint-Louverture (*fran-SWAH doh-min-EEK too-SAHNT low-vuh-CHURE*), a former enslaved person, led a revolt to free Santo Domingo from Spain. He had invaded Santo Domingo from neighboring Haiti. In 1804, Toussaint-Louverture had led a successful revolt against the French.

In Cuba and Puerto Rico, the situation was much different. These Caribbean colonies depended on Spain to buy their sugar and other farm products. In Cuba, there were many more enslaved people than there were *plantation* owners. The plantation owners feared that the slaves would rise up and kill them. The powerful people in government and the wealthy plantation owners did not support revolution in Cuba. Spain could easily defend Cuba and Puerto Rico from attack by other nations. This included defending against possible revolutionaries who might want to travel to Cuba or Puerto Rico.

Cuba and Puerto Rico remained under Spanish control until late in the nineteenth century.

Central American wars of independence (1808–1823)

Wars fought by Central American territories to gain independence from **Spain** (see p. 39). The Napoleonic Wars and revolution in Spain caused Spain to weaken its hold on the Central American colonies in the Kingdom of Guatemala. Guatemala included the territory from what is now the state of Chiapas, **Mexico** (see p. 62), to the nation of Costa Rica.

The colonists in Central America had many complaints about the Spanish government. Like wealthy *Creoles* in other colonies,

During the first twenty-five years of the nineteenth century, most former Spanish colonies in the Americas gained their independence. The map above lists the dates of independence for each present-day nation.

the Creoles in Central America felt that Spain favored those who had been born in Spain. Furthermore, taxes in Central America had increased because of the Napoleonic Wars. Despite these complaints, the government remained loyal to Spain. It tried to avoid rebellion by reforming some of the laws.

The wars for independence started more slowly in Central America for two reasons. First, a strong leader named José de Bustamante y Guerra (*ho-SAY duh bus-tuh-MEN-tay ee GARE-uh*) headed the government of Guatemala. Guatemala was the largest and strongest of the Spanish colonies in Central America. Second, wealthy Creoles were afraid that efforts toward independence would cause Native Americans to rise up and kill the Creoles. Despite these obstacles, rebels did try to start a revolution. Rebel forces fought in San Salvador, Nicaragua, and Guatemala.

In 1814, King Ferdinand VII overturned the Constitution of Cádiz. This so angered the Creoles that they started to support the independence movement. It was not until the Plan of Iguala (see **Mexican War of Independence**, p. 84) was presented that the Creoles fully supported independence. In 1821, the Central American Kingdom of Guatemala declared independence from Spain. In 1823, Guatemala separated into states and nations. Each had its own constitution and laws. These states and nations joined together to create the United Provinces of Central America, which included Guatemela, El Salvador, Honduras, Nicaragua, and Costa Rica. The state of Chiapas remained part of **Mexico** (see p. 62). Panama had joined the Republic of Colombia in 1821.

Florida, East and West

Territory in southeast North America where there has been a strong Spanish influence since the 16th century. During the **American Revolution** (see p. 79), the British briefly held parts of the Florida territory. After the British lost the war, that territory passed once again to **Spain** (see p. 39).

The territory included two parts, East Florida and West Florida. East Florida included what is now the state of Florida, from its southern tip to the city of Tallahassee. West Florida extended from Tallahassee to New Orleans. West Florida also included the southern coastal lands of present-day Mississippi and Alabama and the southeastern corner of Louisiana.

A problem arose over the exact location of the border between West Florida and the United States. Spain felt it had a right to the territory it had won from the British during the American Revolutionary War. This territory extended along the eastern Mississippi River all the way to the Ohio and Tennessee Rivers. The United States did not agree with Spain's claim. American settlers moved into the area in large numbers. In 1810, these settlers rebelled against Spanish rule. The settlers created an independent republic. The United States then annexed, or added, this area to the United States. Spain strongly protested this action.

In 1812, war again erupted between the United States and England. Spain allowed the English to use Pensacola, Florida, as

Spain's territory of West Florida stretched all the way to the Mississippi River. In 1819, the Spanish sold both East and West Florida to the United States.

a naval base. The American general Andrew Jackson led his forces into Pensacola and drove out the English. After the War of 1812, Jackson once again led American troops into Florida during the First Seminole War. (See **War of 1812**, p. 92 and the **First Seminole War**, see p. 89.) The Americans refused to leave Florida, even after the wars had ended.

Spain had a tough decision. It could either declare war on the United States, or it could give up the Florida territories. In 1819, when this decision needed to be made, Spain was greatly weakened from battles in the Napoleonic Wars and the Peninsular War. Much of Spanish America was in rebellion. Spain did not believe it would be able to support a war with the United States. Spain chose to give up the Florida territories. In 1819, Spain signed the Adams-Onís Treaty with the United States.

Louisiana

Territory that stretched from the Mississippi River on its eastern border to the Rocky Mountains in the west. Its southern border was the coast of Louisiana, and it also included land all the way to the Canadian border. The Louisiana Territory served as an important buffer zone between the expanding United States and northern **New Spain** (see p. 67). The French had first claimed this territory in the sixteenth century. In 1762, they lost the land to **Spain** (see p. 39). In 1800, Napoléon Bonaparte forced King Charles IV of Spain to return Louisiana to France.

In 1803, Napoléon decided to sell the territory to the United States. He sold all 828,000 square miles for $15 million, or about

Between 1762 and 1803, the Louisiana Territory was held by France, Spain, then France again, before American president Thomas Jefferson purchased it from France's Napoléon Bonaparte, making it part of the United States.

Although a Creole, Father Hidalgo wanted an independent Mexico that would benefit all of its peoples. He fought for an end to slavery and to forcing Native Americans to pay tribute. (Library of Congress)

three cents per acre. The purchase of this territory doubled the size of the United States.

It also meant that the western border of the United States was now right next to the northeastern border of **New Spain** (see p. 67). This made Spain very uncomfortable. Spain feared that the United States would continue to expand its claims into Spanish territory. By the middle of the nineteenth century, Spain's fears were realized.

Mexican War of Independence (1810-1821)

Series of battles to secure **Mexico's** (see p. 62) independence from **Spain** (see p. 39). The first phase of the Mexican War of Independence was started by a Creole priest in 1810. Father Miguel Hidalgo y Costilla rang the church bells in the village of Dolores, calling the villagers to revolution. He said that the purpose of the revolution was to end slavery. It was also to end the unfair taxes forced on Native Americans by wealthy colonists. Hidalgo also wanted the Native Americans' land restored to them. Father Hidalgo's army included poor **mestizos** (see p. 62) and

Native Americans. They did not have guns or swords. They made weapons from knives, stones, sticks, and large, heavy knives called "machetes" (*mash-ET-ays*). Hidalgo led his rebels from town to town. They opened jails to allow the prisoners to join them. The rebels destroyed the houses of the wealthy people who had been born in Spain. Sometimes Hidalgo's angry mob did not show mercy. They murdered some of the people who surrendered. This rebel army of the poor was very disorganized. In 1811, they had an opportunity to capture Mexico City. Had they done so, their rebellion might have been successful. Instead, they turned away and went to Guadalajara. Father Hidalgo's army was defeated in an important battle near a bridge in Calderón (*call-der-OWN*). The "loyalists," the army that was loyal to Spain, captured Father Hidalgo and executed him.

José María Morelos y Pavón (*ho-SAY muh-REE-uh mor-AY-os ee pah-VON*) continued Hidalgo's efforts. Like Hidalgo,

Fighting for the Equality of All People

One of the aims of the Mexican War of Independence was to end the inequality in rights between people of wealth and the poor. Since the poor were often also of mixed races, the revolutionary effort helped to win fair treatment for all races. Shortly after Mexico won its independence from Spain in 1821, Vincent Guerrero wrote about these goals. In this excerpt, he reminds the newly freed people of Mexico of what has been achieved.

We have defeated the colossus and we bathe in the glow of new found happiness. . . . [We now know] the way to genuine freedom . . . which is to live with a knowledge that no one is above anyone else, that there is no title more honored than that of the citizen, and that applies to the person in the military, a private worker, a government official, a **cleric**, a land owner, a laborer, a craftsman, or a writer . . . because the sacred belief in equality has leveled us before the law.

◀ **cleric**
priest

Morelos y Pavón was a priest. However, Morelos y Pavón was a mestizo, not a Creole like Hidalgo. He led small bands of revolutionaries in quick attacks against the loyalist forces. Using these tactics, he was able to gain control of a large area around Mexico City. In 1813, his forces captured Acapulco. Morelos y Pávon called together a group known as the Congress of Chilpancingo (*chill-pahn-SING-oh*). These revolutionaries wrote Mexico's first formal declaration of independence from Spain. They also wrote a **constitution**. The constitution was important because it abolished class distinctions. This means that a person's rights before the law did not depend on whether that person was an upper-class Creole or a poor mestizo. The constitution was never enforced. Loyalist forces overcame Morelos's army. In 1815, they captured and executed him.

Vicente Guerrero continued the **guerrilla** attacks that Morelos had started. However, loyalist forces were extremely powerful. The fight for Mexico's independence began to falter. In 1820, the revolution in Spain restored the Constitution of Cádiz. This caused many wealthy **Creoles** to switch their loyalties. They started to support the fight for Mexico's independence. One of their important leaders was Colonel Augustín de Iturbide.

Iturbide met with Guerrero in 1821. Together, they created the Plan of Iguala. This plan outlined a structure for Mexico's independence. According to the plan, Mexico would have a king whose power would be limited. The plan promised that all Mexicans would be equal before the law regardless of their race. Property rights would also be protected. The plan also made Roman Catholicism the official religion of the state of Mexico.

Both the wealthy and the poor liked what the Plan of Iguala offered. They accepted it. Soon, there was very little support left for the loyalist cause. In 1821, the Treaty of Córdoba was signed. The treaty declared Mexico's independence from Spain. After three hundred years, **New Spain** (see p. 67) no longer existed.

Monroe Doctrine

American declaration limiting the power of Europe in the Northern Hemisphere. The Monroe **Doctrine** was part of President James Monroe's message to the United States Congress in 1823. There were four parts to the Monroe Doctrine. One part

Treaty of San Lorenzo

East and West Florida were Spain's reward for helping the American revolutionaries in their war of independence from Great Britain. Spain already held the vast territory of Louisiana that was west of the Mississippi River. Spain did not allow the ships of any other nation to travel the Mississippi. Spain also claimed land east of the Mississippi as far north as the Ohio River. By 1795, Spain was facing a period of unrest. The French Revolution had caused Spain to join with other European countries in fighting the new French Republic. With its large holdings in North America, Spain depended on good relations with the newly formed United States. This agreement between the Spanish and United States governments identified the borders between the two nations. Spain agreed to move its northern boundary farther south. Spain also agreed to allow U.S. ships to travel the Mississippi. The United States recognized Spain's claims in Florida.

His Catholic Majesty and the United States of America . . . have determined to establish by a convention several points. . . . To prevent all disputes on the subject of the boundaries which separate the territories of the two . . . Parties, it is hereby declared and agreed as follows: . . . the Southern boundary of the United States which divides their territory from the Spanish Colonies of East and West Florida, shall be designated by a line beginning on the River Mississippi at the Northernmost part of the thirty first degree of latitude North of the Equator which from thence shall be drawn due east to the middle of the River Apalachicola or Catahouche, thence along the middle thereof to its junction with the Flint, thence straight to the head of St. Mary's River, and thence down the middle thereof to the Atlantic Ocean. And it is agreed that if there should be any troops, garrisons or settlements of either party in the territory of the other according to the above mentioned boundaries, they shall be withdrawn from the said territory within the term of six months after the ratification of this treaty or sooner . . . and that they shall be permitted to take with them all the goods and effects which they possess.

stated that the Old World and the *New World* had different approaches to government. Because of this, the two had to remain separate. By 1823, many colonies in the New World had won independence from the European nations that had once controlled them. The United States had some concerns that the European nations might try to take back their colonies. The United States wanted to prevent this. The Monroe Doctrine stated that the European nations could no longer claim land in the Western Hemisphere. This meant that the newly independent Latin American countries would not have to worry about Spain trying to reclaim its lost colonies. In return, the United States promised to stay out of the affairs of these European countries.

Proclamation to the People of Venezuela

In June 1813, Simón Bolívar was leading revolutionary forces toward the Venezuelan capital of Caracas. Bolívar's revolutionary army defeated the Spanish loyalists in battle after battle. Bolívar wanted the people of Venezuela to support the rebels and to help throw off Spanish rule. He wrote a letter to them about this. In this excerpt, Bolívar outlines the sufferings of the Venezuelan people at the hands of the Spanish. He tells the people that the Spanish must be forced to leave.

Moved by your misfortunes, we have been unable to observe with indifference the afflictions you were forced to experience by the barbarous Spaniards, who have ravished you, plundered you, and brought you death and destruction. They have violated the sacred rights of nations. They have broken the most solemn agreements and treaties. In fact, they have committed every manner of crime, reducing the Republic of Venezuela to the most frightful desolation. Justice therefore demands vengeance, and necessity compels us to exact it. Let the monsters who infest Colombian soil, who have drenched it in blood, be cast out forever; may their punishment be the equal to the enormity of their **perfidy**, so that we may eradicate the stain of our **ignominy** and demonstrate to the nations of the world that the sons of America cannot be offended with **impunity**.

◀ **perfidy**
deliberate violation of trust

◀ **ignominy**
dishonor

◀ **impunity**
exemption from punishment

Santo Domingo

Eastern part of the Caribbean island of Hispaniola. Santo Domingo was Spain's first colony in the *New World*. Bartolomeo Columbus, the brother of explorer **Christopher Columbus** (see p. 52), founded Santo Domingo in 1496. It remained a Spanish colony until 1795 when **Spain** (see p. 39) was forced to give the colony to the French. The French controlled Santo Domingo until 1809 when it was returned to Spain. In 1821, the Haitian revolutionary leader François-Dominique Toussaint Louverture invaded Santo Domingo, then declared the colony's independence from Spain. Santo Domingo remained under Haitian control until 1844, when it won its own independence and became a separate nation. The loss of Santo Domingo was particularly upsetting to the Spanish. It was historically important to the Spanish Empire since it had been Spain's first major success in the New World.

Simón Bolívar was one of the most important revolutionary leaders in South America's fight for independence from Spain. (Library of Congress)

Seminole War, First

First of three wars fought between the United States and the Seminole Native American nation. After the **American Revolution** (see p. 79), Britain was forced to give **Florida** (see p. 82) back to **Spain** (see p. 39). New settlers rushed in to claim land in Florida. The settlers included Spanish colonists, Americans, and Seminole Native Americans. American settlers in what is now Georgia wanted the land owned by the Spanish and the Seminoles.

In 1817, U.S. troops, under the command of General Andrew Jackson, invaded **East Florida** (see p. 82). Jackson claimed that the Seminole Native Americans had attacked some Georgia homesteads and killed the people there. He wanted to punish the Seminole. The Seminole land had also become a place where runaway enslaved peoples could hide. Jackson wanted to return these enslaved peoples to the United States. The Spanish governor protested the presence of the American soldiers. Jackson insisted the soldiers had a right to be there. He captured St. Marks in April 1818. Jackson's army then captured the city of Pensacola. This gave the United States control over East Florida, even though Spain owned it. In 1819, the Adams-Onís Treaty gave all of Florida to the United States.

South American wars of independence (1806-1826)

The South American wars of independence moved in two directions. Efforts to free the South American colonies from **Spain** (see p. 39) started at the same time in two different places. In the north, Simón Bolívar led armies against the Spanish in what is now Venezuela. In the south, José de San Martín led the revolutionaries in what are now Argentina, Bolivia, Paraguay, and Uruguay.

The battles for South American independence started in 1806 when Francisco de Miranda, known as "The Forerunner," led a revolution in Venezuela. For a short time, he became the dictator of this new country. The Spanish soon took Venezuela back from the rebels, and Miranda escaped.

In 1808, Simón Bolívar began the work of independence for Venezuela. By 1810, the Spanish governor of Venezuela had been forced to resign. In 1811, Venezuela's national congress declared independence. Bolívar served in the army of the new republic of Venezuela. Spain continued to fight for its colony despite the decision of the Venezuelan congress. Spain won back control of Venezuela in 1812.

By 1813, Bolívar was back in Venezuela. He captured the capital city of Caracas and was given the title "Liberator." The Spanish returned once again and defeated Bolívar in 1814. In 1815, Spain sent a large army to South America to defeat the revolutionary armies. For four years, Bolívar battled the Spanish armies throughout the region. In 1819, he developed a plan for a final victory over the Spanish.

Bolívar led a small army through floods, icy mountains, and land that seemed almost impassable. He took his men to New Granada in what is now Colombia. The Spanish did not believe anyone could travel that route. Bolívar took them completely by surprise in the Battle of Boyacá (*boy-AY-ka*). Three days later, he entered the city of Bogotá (*BO-gah-tah*).

At Bolívar's urging, the Republic of Gran Colombia was created. This was a union of Venezuela, Colombia, and Panama. In 1820, the Spanish made one more attempt to take back Venezuela. They were defeated in the Battle of Carabobo (*car-uh-BO-bo*) in 1821. Venezuela became an independent nation.

In 1822, Bolívar turned his attention to Ecuador. His lieutenant, Antonio José de Sucre, won an important victory in the Battle of Pichincha (*peesh-EEN-cha*). Ecuador then joined the Republic of Gran Colombia.

At the same time that Bolívar was leading the revolutionary armies from north to south, another famous general was leading revolutionary armies from south to north. José de San Martín was pushing the Spanish forces out of the viceroyalty of La Plata. This area included what are now Argentina, Bolivia, Paraguay, and Uruguay. By 1813, most forces loyal to Spain had been driven out of La Plata. In 1816, La Plata declared its independence from Spain. San Martín pushed forward into Chile in 1817. His armies defeated the Spanish forces at Casas de Chacabuco (*CAHS-us duh cha-cuh-BOO-coh*). San Martín captured the city of Santiago, Chile. It took him one more year to drive the rest of the loyalist armies out of Chile. He achieved this through the important victory at the Battle of Maipú in 1818.

In 1820, San Martín moved into Peru. He captured the capital city of Lima in 1821. With this victory, San Martín declared Peru's independence from Spain. The forces loyal to Spain continued to resist. San Martín needed help. He met with Simón Bolívar, and they planned a final military action in Peru. In 1824, Bolívar won the Battle of Ayacucho. This was the last important battle in the South American wars of independence. By 1826, the last Spanish forces were driven out of Peru.

Texas

Northeastern border territory of the Republic of **Mexico** (see p. 62). In the Adams-Onís Treaty, the United States had agreed that Texas was part of **New Spain** (see p. 67). When Mexico won independence from Spain in 1821 (see **Mexican War of Independence**, p. 84), Texas became part of the Republic of Mexico. Texas was the most northeastern part of the new republic. It bordered the **Louisiana Territory** (see p. 60) that the United States had purchased from France in 1803.

vaquero

Hispanic cowboy. *Vaqueros* (*vah-KARE-os*) were talented horsemen. Throughout the nineteenth century, vaqueros worked on cattle ranches in **Mexico** (see p. 62), **New Mexico** (see p. 66), and

Texas (see p. 91). Their main job was to round up and brand cattle, but they were skilled in many areas of horsemanship. The vaqueros had contests every year to demonstrate their skills. The contests were called *rodeos*.

The vaqueros introduced many useful things to English-speaking cowboys. The vaqueros showed the cowboys how to use a knotted rope, called a *lasso*, to catch cattle. Vaqueros also wore special clothing that was very well suited to their work. They used the *sombrero*, a wide-brimmed hat, to keep the sun out of their eyes. Leather pants, called *chaps*, protected their legs while riding through high brush. The vaqueros also introduced a type of saddle that rose higher in the front and back. This saddle made it easier to stay on horseback while roping cattle. The saddle style is still in use today. It is called the *Western saddle*.

War of 1812 (1812-1814)

War between England and the United States over the rights of American ships at sea. The United States considered itself a neutral power during the Napoleonic Wars that involved France and England. This means that the United States was not an ally of either France or England. France had agreed that the United States could continue to trade with England without interference from the French navy. The English, however, did not keep a similar agreement. Britain continued to restrict U.S. ships from doing trade with France. This hurt American business.

Britain was also helping the Shawnee Native American leader Tecumseh in his battles with United States. American settlers continued to move onto Shawnee land despite U.S. government's promises that they would not do this.

The United States declared war on England in 1812. The United States fought England at the Canadian border. The English prepared to attack New Orleans in **Louisiana** (see p. 83). They were able to do this because the Spanish allowed the English to use Pensacola, **Florida** (see p. 82), as a naval base.

In 1814, the United States general Andrew Jackson captured Pensacola from the English. The U.S. forces kept control of Pensacola. This eventually led to the Adams-Onís Treaty in 1819.

CHAPTER FOUR

Manifest Destiny

The Texan Revolution and the U.S.-Mexican War, 1824–1848

"[It is the United States's] manifest destiny to overspread the continent allotted by Providence for the free development of our yearly multiplying millions."

—John L. O'Sullivan, editor of *United States Magazine and Democratic Review*, 1845

In 1821, **Mexico** (see p. 62) won independence from **Spain** (see p. 39). All the territory in North and Central America that had been part of the Spanish colonies was now part of the Republic of Mexico. This territory included vast regions of North America. The northernmost area of these lands was called the "**Far North**" (see p. 106). It included present-day **California** (see p. 104), Arizona, **New Mexico** (see p. 66), **Texas** (see p. 91), and Nevada. Parts of Colorado, Wyoming, Utah, Kansas, and Oklahoma also were in the Far North. The Far North was a huge area for Mexico to try to govern, especially from as far away as Mexico City.

Although the North American territories were so far away, Mexico valued them greatly. The Far North provided huge tracts of land where the Republic of Mexico could expand. It also acted as a buffer between Mexico and the United States. Mexico did not trust the United States when it came to territory. The Mexicans had seen that the United States was determined to expand its territory as far as possible. Mexico wanted to ensure that the Far North was protected. The Mexican government depended on its colonists to control the Far North territories.

The Mexican government used the Spanish-speaking Hispanic

colonists to help manage the areas in which the colonists lived. In California, these colonists were called *Californios* (*cal-i-FORN-yos*). In New Mexico, the colonists called themselves *Nuevomexicanos* (*NWAY-voh may-he-KAHN-os*) Hispanic colonists who lived in Texas were called *Tejanos* (*tay-HAHN-os*). Not all of the Far North territories had Hispanic communities. Very few Hispanic colonists lived in Utah or Nevada. The Hispanic colonists in California, New Mexico, and Texas considered themselves Mexican citizens. They had more freedom than some other Mexican citizens because they were so far away from the main government in Mexico City. They became used to making more of their own decisions to suit the area in which they lived. The colonists had more contact with people from other nations. In California, ships from all over the world came to trade. The Santa Fe Trail brought traders from the United States to Mexico. Texas's border with the United States allowed many U.S. citizens to come easily into Texas to trade or to settle. In fact, many settlers came with the traders to these areas.

Mexico encouraged settlers from the United States to come into the Far North. The settlers from the United States were sometimes given land grants by the Mexican government. The government hoped that the new settlers would learn Hispanic traditions and language. The settlers would then become Mexican citizens. In the 1820s, most of the Hispanic colonists in California, New Mexico, and Texas welcomed the new settlers. They felt the U.S. settlers would help these areas prosper. More people meant that more of

Timeline

1824

The Mexican Constitution of 1824 is adopted. Part of the Constitution says that Mexican citizens of all races are equal under the law.

1829

Antonio Armijo completes the **Spanish Trail**. This opens up trade from Santa Fe to **California**.

Mexico outlaws slavery. This causes disagreement among some Texans who own enslaved peoples.

the land would be used. This would benefit everyone.

By the 1830s, however, there were many more U.S. settlers than the Mexican government wanted. Some areas had more U.S. settlers than Hispanic colonists. Also, the settlers were not behaving as the Mexican government expected. They refused to become Mexican citizens. They often ignored Mexican laws. They mistreated Hispanic colonists. The U.S. settlers began to act as if the land they settled had belonged to them all along. They believed they had a right to take the land they wanted, even though it really belonged to someone else.

The Mexican government was disorganized. Two groups were fighting over how the government should function. This made it harder for Mexico to pay attention to the Hispanic colonists and U.S. settlers in the Far North. As a result, the government couldn't respond quickly enough to stop trouble.

Texas was the first area of the Far North to cause a serious problem for Mexico. Beginning in the 1820s, U.S. settlers poured into Texas. By the mid-1830s, there were ten people from the United States for every Tejano. The settlers lived by their own rules. They ignored Mexican laws. They offended the Tejano colonists with their behavior. The U.S. settlers looked down on the Tejano residents of Texas. Many Tejano residents looked down on the U.S. settlers as well. However, there were many more U.S. settlers than Tejano residents. Racism was common. This is the belief that people of one race are superior to people of another race. Some of the Anglo-American settlers in Texas believed they were superior to Native Americans, Africans, and

1829	**1830**	**1833**	**1835**
General Antonio López de Santa Anna defeats the Spanish forces trying to invade Mexico. Santa Anna becomes the "Hero of Tampico."	Mexico passes a law that closes the border to settlers between the United States and Texas.	**Antonio López de Santa Anna** becomes president of Mexico. Texans send **Stephen Austin** to Mexico City. He tries to persuade the Mexican government to make Texas an independent state within the Republic of Mexico.	Texas declares independence from Mexico. **Texan Revolution** begins. Siege of San Antonio de Béxar (October–December); Texan forces take San Antonio.

Mexicans. Soon, many settlers believed that Mexico, and Mexicans, should not own Texas. They believed it was their right to take Texas away from Mexico.

The government in Mexico tried to stop U.S. settlers from coming into Texas. They passed laws, hoping that the situation in Texas would change. They closed the border, but the settlers ignored the law and came anyway. Mexico tried to enforce a law that prohibited slavery in the Republic of Mexico. Many of the U.S. settlers from the South had brought enslaved people with them. The settlers ignored that law, too. They wanted their own laws, not Mexico's. They wanted more freedom to do as they chose within Texas. Finally, they wanted Texas to become an independent nation.

Some Tejanos agreed with the U.S. settlers. The disorganization in the Mexican government led a group of Tejanos to side with the settlers. The Tejanos felt that Texas would be a better place to live if it were not under Mexico's control. Even though many U.S. settlers mistreated them, the Tejanos believed things would improve once Texas was free of Mexico. The disagreements between the people of Texas and the Mexican government led to the **Texan Revolution** (see p. 120) in 1835. Within a year, Texas had won independence from Mexico. It became the Republic of Texas.

After the Texan Revolution, the Mexican government paid closer attention to its other territories in the Far North. It did not want to lose California or New Mexico as it had lost Texas. Mexico tried to pass laws to prevent more U.S. settlers from coming into California and New Mexico. It was too late.

1836	1836	1837	1841
General Antonio López de Santa Anna's army defeats the Texans in a series of bloody battles. Texan rage at Santa Anna's actions results in the battle cry, "Remember the Alamo."	Texans under **Sam Houston** surprise Santa Anna's army and defeat it at the Battle of San Jacinto. Santa Anna signs treaty recognizing Texan independence. Houston is elected first president of the Republic of Texas.	Mexican citizens of **New Mexico** begin revolt against unjust governorship of Albino Pérez. Disgraced by the defeat at San Jacinto, **General Antonio López de Santa Anna** is forced out of office as president of Mexico.	John Tyler becomes U.S. president following the death of William Harrison.

There were already signs by the early 1840s that the U.S. settlers in California were feeling just as the Texans had felt in 1835. They looked down on the Hispanic colonists, the Californios. Like the Texans, the U.S. settlers in California felt they had the right to take away the land from Mexico.

The U.S. government under President James Polk encouraged the U.S. settlers in California. Like many other Americans, Polk believed in **Manifest Destiny** (see p. 109), the notion that the United States has a "natural right" to all the lands of North America. The Republic of Mexico held most of these lands. From 1821 to 1846, different U.S. presidents tried to buy the land from Mexico. Mexico always refused. Hispanic peoples had settled on this land, and Mexico did not want to give it up. Still, the United States persisted. Once again, Texas was the trouble spot.

Texas had tried to become part of the United States almost from the time Texas had won independence from Mexico in 1835. Mexico had never really recognized this independence. One of the main issues was the location of the border between Texas and Mexico. The Mexican government was not in a position to do much about the problem, so it ignored it. When the United States agreed to make Texas a state in 1845, the Mexican government protested. Mexico felt that the addition of Texas to the United States was simple theft. To the Mexican government, the United States had stolen land that belonged to Mexico. It stopped communication with the United States. President Polk knew this would happen. The United States and Mexico were on the edge of war.

1844	**1845**	**1846**	**1846**
James K. Polk elected U.S. president.	Texas becomes the twenty-eighth state in the United States.	**U.S.-Mexican War begins**.	Mexican captain Juan Flóres leads revolt against U.S. forces in Los Angeles.
	Magazine editor first uses the phrase, "**Manifest Destiny**" to justify U.S. expansion in the West.	California declares independence from Mexico in the **Bear Flag Revolt**.	
		U.S. force under General Zachary Taylor defeats General **Santa Anna's** army at Monterey.	

Polk sent part of the U.S. army to the border between Texas and Mexico. He sent them to the Rio Grande River. This was the border Texas claimed. Mexico said that the border was farther north, at the Nueces River. As far as Mexico was concerned, the United States had invaded Mexico by sending U.S. troops to the Rio Grande. Mexico responded by sending an army to meet the U.S. forces. Polk knew this would happen when he sent the U.S. army to the Rio Grande. The United States had pushed Mexico into war.

The **U.S.-Mexican War** (see p. 124) lasted from 1846 to 1848. One of the soldiers in that war was a young Ulysses S. Grant. He would become president of the United States after the Civil War. He said that the U.S.-Mexican War was unjust. He said that the United States had pushed Mexico into defending itself. The United States was sure it would win any war it started with Mexico. If the United States won the war, it would gain the territory that it had so long desired.

The United States did win the war. On February 2, 1848, the United States and Mexico signed the **Treaty of Guadalupe Hidalgo** (see p. 122). The treaty gave the United States all the territory in the Far North that it been trying to get for years. This new territory gave the United States much of the shape it has today. A large part of the territory that Mexico gave up became the American Southwest. This was the area with the greatest number of Hispanic colonists. It was in the American Southwest that the Hispanic American culture of today began to put down its U.S. roots.

1847

U.S. forces under General Zachary Taylor defeat the Mexican army at Buena Vista.

Troops under General Winfield Scott defeat Mexicans at the fort of Veracruz. This opens the way to Mexico City for the United States.

1847

The United States captures castle and military academy at Chapultepec. Mexican cadets fight to the death rather than surrender. They are remembered as "Los Heroes Niños."

U.S. Army under General Winfield Scott captures Mexico City

1848

Treaty of Guadalupe Hidalgo ends the U.S.-Mexican War. Mexico gives the United States its territories in the Far North, including California and New Mexico, and much of Arizona, Colorado, Utah, and Nevada.

A-Z of Key People, Places and Terms

Alamo, Battle of the (1836)

Battle of **Texan Revolution** (see p. 120). **General Antonio López de Santa Anna** (see p. 113) wanted revenge on the rebel Texans after the Mexican army's loss at the Siege of Béxar. He led an army of about four thousand soldiers into San Antonio. Most of the Texan army had already left the area. A small number of rebels remained. They gathered in an abandoned **mission** (see p. 64) called the Alamo.

The Alamo was a strong fort. There was no roof but the walls were ten feet high and three feet thick. Only about 190 Texans were in the Alamo. Colonel William B. Travis commanded the Texans. Jim Bowie and Davy Crockett were with him. Jim Bowie was the person who invented the bowie knife used for hunting.

The Alamo (Library of Congress)

Santa Anna's View

The defeat at the Alamo was a serious blow to the Texans rebelling against Mexico. The deaths of the Alamo defenders angered the Texans and made them fight even harder. To the Mexican government, however, the defenders of the Alamo posed a threat to Mexico. The Texan rebels were seen as criminals, not heroes. The Mexicans viewed the Texan Revolution as an attempt by bad people to steal what rightfully belonged to Mexico. After the fall of the Alamo, General Antonio López de Santa Anna sent a letter to the people of Texas. In this letter, dated March 6, 1836, Santa Anna gives the Mexicans' point of view of the war between Mexico and Texas.

The General-in-Chief of the Army of Operations of the Mexican Republic, to the inhabitants of Texas:

Citizens! The causes which have conducted to this frontier a part of the Mexican Army are not unknown to you, a parcel of audacious adventurers, maliciously protected by some inhabitants of a neighboring republic dared to invade our territory, with the intention of dividing amongst themselves the fertile lands that are contained in the spacious Department of Texas; and even had the boldness to entertain the idea of reaching the capital of the republic. It became necessary to check and chastise such enormous daring; and in consequence, some exemplary punishments have already taken place . . . I am pained to find amongst those adventurers the names of some colonists, to whom had been granted repeated benefits, and who had no motive of complaint against the government of their adopted country. These ungrateful men must also necessarily suffer the just punishment that the laws and the public vengeance demand. But if we are bound to punish the criminal, we are not the less compelled to protect the innocent. It is thus that the inhabitants of this country, let their origin be what it may, who should not appear to have been implicated in such iniquitous rebellion, shall be respected in their persons and property, provided they come forward and report themselves to the commander of the troops within eight days after they should have arrived in their respective settlements, in order to justify their conduct and to receive a document guaranteeing to them the right of enjoying that which lawfully belongs to them.

Béxarians! Return to your homes and dedicate yourselves to your domestic duties. Your city and the fortress of the Alamo are already in possession of the Mexican Army, composed of your own fellow citizens; and rest assured that no mass of foreigners will ever interrupt your repose, and much less, attack your lives and plunder your property. The Supreme Government has taken you under its protection and will seek for your good.

Davy Crockett was a former U.S. congressman from Tennessee. Bowie and Crockett had come to Texas to help the Texans win independence from Mexico. There were also some Tejanos (*tay-HAHN-ohs*) in the Alamo. These Tejanos, such as **Juan Seguín** (see p. 117), supported the **Texan Revolution** (see p. 120). The Texans also included some women and children.

The Texans did not have very many soldiers but they had about twenty cannons. They hoped that the cannons would help defend the Alamo long enough for help to come from the other Texan rebels. Colonel Travis had sent Juan Seguín to find the Texan forces.

General Santa Anna surrounded the Alamo with the Mexican army. He raised a red flag. This was a signal to the defenders of the Alamo that they must surrender immediately. If they refused, they would be captured and killed. The Texans replied to this threat by firing their cannons into the ranks of the Mexican army. It was February 23, 1846; the Battle of the Alamo had begun.

For thirteen days, the Mexicans and Texans fired on each other. In the early morning of March 6, Santa Anna ordered eighteen hundred of his men to storm the walls of the Alamo. The Texans fired their cannons to try to stop the Mexican soldiers. After the third try, some of the Mexican soldiers managed to climb over the Alamo's high walls. They opened a gate. The rest of the attacking Mexican soldiers poured into the Alamo.

Within a short time, most of the Texan soldiers that remained in the Alamo had been killed. General Santa Anna did not harm the women and children he found in the Alamo. He released them, and they passed safely through the Mexican lines.

General Santa Anna was happy to have defeated the Texan rebels at the Alamo. When word of the Alamo reached the other Texans, however, it only made them even more determined to win independence. "Remember the Alamo" became the battle cry of the Texans.

Armijo, Manuel

Governor of **New Mexico** (see p. 66) while the territory was held by the Republic of **Mexico** (see p. 62). Manuel Armijo (*man-WELL arm-EE-ho*) was a wealthy sheep rancher in what is now New Mexico. The Mexican government appointed him governor of the territory of New Mexico in 1827. He served fewer than eighteen months. After the **New Mexican Rebellion** (see p. 110) in 1837, Armijo again became governor. He replaced General Albino Pérez who had been killed in the rebellion. Armijo's treatment of the people of New Mexico was as harsh as Pérez's had been.

In 1841, Armijo discovered that an *expedition* from **Texas** (see p. 91) had been sent to Santa Fe. They were trying to see if the people in the northeastern area of New Mexico would fight to become part of the Republic of Texas. Governor Armijo and the Mexican government saw this as an invasion. Armijo pulled together a *militia* to fight off the expedition. The Texans were captured and sent to prisons in Mexico.

In 1846, the war between the United States and Mexico began. Brigadier General Stephen Watts Kearny was the U.S. commander of the Army of the West. His goal was to capture **New Mexico** (see p. 66). He marched his army over a thousand miles along the **Santa Fe Trail** (see p. 114). Kearny's forces captured Santa Fe. There was no resistance from the Mexicans in New Mexico. Armijo had gathered a militia but it never met Kearny's forces in battle.

Austin, Stephen (1793-1836)

Stephen Austin (Library of Congress)

Texas (see p. 91) statesman and founder of Anglo-American settlements in Texas. Stephen Austin was raised in the territory of Missouri. In 1819, his father developed a plan to colonize Texas. The Mexican government gave his father a land grant. Austin's father died before he could begin. Stephen carried out his father's project. In 1822, he founded a colony of several hundred families. They settled along the Bravos River.

By the 1830s, many more settlers had moved into Texas. Austin became a leader among the Texans. In 1833, he went to **Mexico** (see p. 62) to persuade the Mexicans to allow Texas to become a separate state within the Republic of Mexico. The Texans wanted their own laws and government. Austin failed to win Mexican support. He then suggested that the Texans organize themselves as a separate state without waiting for Mexico to agree. When the Mexican government heard of this plan, they put Austin in prison.

Austin was released from Mexico in 1835 and returned to Texas. When the **Texan Revolution** (see p. 120) broke out that same year, he went to the United States to ask for help. The Texans succeeded in defeating the Mexicans and became an independent republic. Austin wanted to be the first president of the Texas Republic. The Texans chose **Samuel Houston** (see p. 107) instead. Austin served briefly as secretary of state for Texas before his death in 1836.

Bear Flag Revolt (1846)

California (see p. 104) settlers' rebellion. As the United States expanded into the West, American settlers made their way to California. Many of the first settlers arrived without families. They married into the native Mexican, Spanish-speaking society in California known as *Californios* (*cal-ee-FORN-yos*). Most of these settlers became citizens of **Mexico** (see p. 63).

The next large group of settlers to the area came in 1840. They came into northern California from the **Oregon Trail** (see p. 111). Unlike the earlier settlers, these settlers brought their families. They believed in the idea of **Manifest Destiny** (see p. 109). Most of the settlers arriving after 1840 refused to become citizens of Mexico. They regarded themselves as citizens of the United States. Many looked down on the Californios and treated them badly. The behavior of these settlers set the stage for the rebellion known as the Bear Flag Revolt.

As the number of Anglo-American settlers in California increased, they began to dislike the fact that California was part of the Republic of Mexico. They demanded that California become independent. The settlers' goal was for California to become part of the United States. By 1846, numerous disagree-

John C. Frémont (Library of Congress)

ments were brewing between the governments of the United States and Mexico. The Anglo-American settlers believed the time had come to fight for California's independence.

On June 4th, 1846, a rebel force led by Captain John C. Frémont marched into Sonoma, north of San Francisco. General Mariano Vallejo (*mahr-ee-AH-noh vall-AY-ho*) was the military commander of northern California under the Mexican government. The rebels arrested him. Frémont forced Vallejo to surrender. The rebels weren't sure if the United States was at war with Mexico, so they couldn't claim the captured territory for the United States. But they decided to declare California's independence from Mexico. They called California the Bear Flag Republic. Their flag showed the outline of a bear. Although they had declared California an independent republic, the rebels really wanted the United States to annex, or add, California to the United States. Once the rebels learned that the United States had declared war on Mexico, they replaced the bear flag with the flag of the United States.

The Bear Flag Revolt was the beginning of a series of actions taken by the United States to separate California from Mexico.

California

Province of **Spain** (see p. 39), and then **Mexico** (see p. 62), until 1848. The Spanish-speaking settlers in the area now known as California saw many changes beginning in 1821. In that year,

Taken Prisoner during the Bear Flag Revolt (1846)

Mariano Guadalupe Vallejo was a wealthy Californio. Despite his wealth, he had always supported the California settlers' desires to break free of Mexico. He was very surprised when he was arrested during the settlers' rebellion in 1846. The rebellion was called the Bear Flag Revolt. In this excerpt, Vallejo describes what happened to him on the day he was arrested.

Gentlemen under Captain Frémont's command took the road leading through the Napa Hills to Sonoma and at dawn on the fourteenth of June they surrounded my house located on the plaza at Sonoma. At daybreak they raised the shout of alarm and when I heard it, I looked out my bedroom window. To my great surprise, I made out groups of armed men scattered to the right and left of my residence. The recent arrivals were not in uniform, but were all armed and presented a fierce aspect. Some of them wore on their heads a visorless cap of coyote skin, some a low-crowned plush hat, [and] some a red cotton handkerchief. . . . I suspected that the intruders had intentions harmful not to my [property] interests alone, but to my life and that of the members of my family. I realized that my situation was desperate. My wife advised me to try and flee by the rear door, but I told her that such a step was unworthy and that under no circumstances could I decide to desert my young family at such a critical time. I had my uniform brought, dressed quickly and then ordered the large vestibule door thrown open. The house was immediately filled with armed men. I went with them into the parlor of my residence. I asked them what the trouble was and who was heading the party, but had to repeat the question a second time, because almost all of those who were in the parlor replied at once, "Here we are all heads." When I again asked to whom I should take this matter up, the pointed out William B. Ide who was the eldest of all. I then addressed that gentleman and informed him that I wanted to know what happy circumstance I owed the visit of so many individuals. In reply he stated that both Captain Merritt and the other gentlemen who were in his company had decided not to continue living any longer under the Mexican government, whose representatives, Castro and Pio Pico, did not respect the rights of American citizens living in the Departamento; that Castro was every once in a while issuing proclamations treating them all as bandits, and, in a desire to put a stop to all of these insults, they had decided to declare California independent; that while he held none but sentiments of regard for me, he would be forced to take me prisoner along with all my family.

Mexico declared its independence from Spain and became the Republic of Mexico.

California ports welcomed traders from around the world. U.S., Russian, French, and British sailors brought goods into California despite the fact that Spain outlawed such trade. After California became part of Mexico, trade was officially opened. Many more ships began to arrive, especially from the United States.

Some of the traders stayed and became settlers in California. Others arrived from the **Oregon Trail** (see p. 111) or the **Spanish Trail** (see p. 119). By 1840, there were many English-speaking settlers from the United States living in California. There were also thousands of Spanish-speaking Mexican settlers, known as *Californios*. Over time, more and more U.S. settlers poured into California. At first, the Californios welcomed them. They felt the settlers would benefit California. After some time, however, the Californios changed their minds. The new settlers did not intend to become Mexican citizens even though California was part of the Republic of Mexico. The new settlers soon talked about making California an independent country. In 1846, these settlers put their ideas into action. They revolted against Mexico during the **Bear Flag Revolt** (see p. 103).

fandango

Traditional Spanish dance. Unlike most of the popular dances of the early nineteenth century, the fandango (*fan-DAN-go*) was fast moving. Men and women danced closely together using quick steps. The fandango was danced to lively music that had both Spanish and Native American influences.

The word *fandango* also described a type of dance party. Fandangos sometimes went on for several days. A variety of Hispanic dances were displayed, including the *jota* (*HO-tuh*) and the *borrego* (*bor-AY-go*). Fandangos were popular on the large Hispanic ranches called *rancherias* (*ranch-er-EE-as*). There were many of these *rancherias* throughout **California** (see p. 104), **New Mexico** (see p. 66), and **Texas** (see p. 91).

Far North

Area of North America that was part of colonial **New Spain** (see

p. 67). **Mexico** (see p. 62) declared its independence from **Spain** (see p. 39) in 1821. The area of New Spain that had been called the Far North then became part of Mexico. The Far North was the northernmost territory of Mexico. It included present-day **California** (see p. 104), Nevada, Utah, Arizona, **New Mexico** (see p. 66), **Texas** (see p. 91), and part of Colorado.

The Mexican government found it difficult to govern this area because it was so far from Mexico City. While the Far North was vast territory, it contained very few Hispanic settlements. Those few settlements were concentrated in areas of California, Arizona, New Mexico, and Texas.

Even though the Far North was difficult to govern, Mexico regarded it as a valuable possession. It offered land for future settlement. It acted as a *buffer* to protect the main part of Mexico from attacks by foreign powers or Native American nations. Mexico did not want to lose the lands of the Far North.

The rapidly expanding United States also valued the Far North territories. Settlers poured into the territories held by Mexico. At first, Mexico welcomed them, but that soon changed. By the 1830s, these settlers had become a real threat to Mexican ownership of the Far North.

Sam Houston (Library of Congress)

Houston, Samuel (1793-1863)

Lawyer, leader in **Texan Revolution** (see p. 120), first president of the Republic of **Texas** (see p. 91). Sam Houston was born in Virginia and grew up in Tennessee. In his mid-teens he ran away and lived with the Cherokee. He learned their customs and language. The Cherokee called him "Black Raven." Living among the Cherokee gave Houston a lifelong sympathy for Native Americans in the United States.

In 1829, Houston left Tennessee and lived once more with the Cherokee. He learned that the government agents who

Sam Houston (center) in white pants in this painting, defeated the Mexican army under General Santa Anna at the Battle of San Jacinto. Santa Anna, who lost his leg in the battle is seen preparing to surrender. (Library of Congress)

were supposed to be helping the Cherokee were actually stealing from them. Houston went to Washington, D.C., to try to resolve this problem. He became good friends with President Andrew Jackson.

In 1832, Jackson asked Houston to go to the Mexican territory of Texas to talk with the Native Americans. Jackson wanted to make an agreement with the Native Americans to stop their attacks on the traders in Texas. When Houston arrived, the settlers there were already starting to challenge the laws of Mexico in Texas. Houston built a home in Texas in 1833. He became a strong leader of the settlers.

In 1835, the Texan Revolution began. Houston was named commander of the Texan army. He fought bravely in many battles. He led the Texans against General Antonio López de Santa Anna during the Battle of San Jacinto (*san HA-seen-toh*). His small force of Texans defeated the much larger Mexican army. General Santa Anna was forced to sign a treaty that recognized Texas as an independent republic. The Texans elected Sam Houston as their first president.

Houston was president of the Republic of Texas (see the **Lone Star Republic**, p. 109) from 1836 until 1838. He was president again from 1841 to 1844. Houston's influence helped Texas become part of the United States in 1845. He continued to serve Texas as a senator up until the Civil War. He lived in Texas until his death. The city of Houston, Texas, is named in his honor.

Lone Star Republic

Name of the independent Republic of **Texas** (see p. 91). The **Texan Revolution** (see p. 120) ended in 1836, and the Republic of Texas was formed. **Sam Houston** (see p. 107) became its first elected president. The Republic was known as the Lone Star Republic, and its flag displayed a single star on a red, white, and blue background. Even though Texas was then an independent republic, its people wanted to join the United States. In 1845, Texas became part of the United States. **Mexico** (see p. 62) had never recognized Texas's independence. It did not recognize the borders that Texas claimed separated it from Mexico. The disagreements between the United States and Mexico about the Texas borders and other borders in the southwest led to war between the United States and Mexico.

Manifest Destiny

Phrase used by leaders and politicians in the 1840s to justify U.S. expansion into the West. In 1845, John L. O'Sullivan, a magazine editor, wrote that it was the "manifest destiny," or obvious "natural right," of the United States to stretch from the Atlantic Ocean in the east to the Pacific Ocean in the west. Many Americans shared O'Sullivan's views. From the time of the earliest American colonies, settlers believed they had a right to the land they settled. As more people came to the United States, government leaders looked westward for more land. The Republic of **Mexico** (see p. 62) held most of this land. American leaders did not want any foreign government to control these regions. American leaders believed it was part of Manifest Destiny for the United States to take control of this territory. This belief led to a great conflict with Mexico. Mexicans did not agree that the United States had the right to land held by Mexico. The disagreement between the two nations led to the **Texan Revolution** (see p. 120) and the **U.S.-Mexican War** (see p. 124).

Navarro, José Antonio (1795–1871)

Texas patriot and legislator. José Antonio Navarro (*Ho-say an-TOH-nee-oh nav-AHR-oh*) was born in the area that later became **Texas** (see p. 91). At the time of his birth, this area was still under the control of **Spain** (see p. 39). At eighteen, Navarro joined the fight for independence from Spain. In 1821, while working and studying law in San Antonio, he and **Stephen Austin** (see p. 102) became friends.

Navarro was elected to the Mexican congress in the late 1820s. He represented Tejanos like himself, Spanish-speaking native Mexicans of Texas. He also represented the Anglo-American colonists in Texas. He believed that the Anglo-American colonists would help Texas grow and would protect it from attacks by Native Americans.

Navarro was a strong supporter of Texan independence. This made him unpopular with other Mexican congressmen. In 1836, Navarro was one of three Mexican legislators to sign the Texas declaration of independence from Mexico. He was then elected to the congress of the Republic of Texas.

In 1841, Navarro joined an expedition to Santa Fe. The purpose of the expedition was to take control of eastern **New Mexico** (see p. 66). It would then become part of the Republic of Texas. The Mexican army captured the expedition. Navarro was imprisoned in Mexico for three years.

When he was released, he returned to Texas as a hero. He had supported Texas's wish to become part of the United States. Texas achieved statehood in 1845. Navarro was a member of the group that produced the Texas state constitution. The people of San Antonio elected him as their first state senator. He spoke out to make sure that the rights of Hispanic Texans were protected. This issue remained one of the most important forces for the rest of Navarro's long life. Today he remains a hero to many Hispanic Americans.

New Mexican Rebellion (1837)

Revolt of Mexican citizens in **New Mexico** (see p. 66) against Mexican government policies. The area that is now New Mexico had been part of the territory called the **Far North** (see p. 106), first by the Spanish, then by the Republic of **Mexico** (see p. 63). When Mexico won its independence, many things changed for the people of Mexico.

One of the things that changed was the rule controlling trade with other countries. The Spanish had tightly controlled who could trade goods in the Spanish territories. The Republic of

Mexico changed the laws to make it easier for the United States and other countries to trade in New Mexico. The new government also passed laws that promised equal rights to all races of Mexican citizens. The laws protected all citizen—rich and poor.

Even though the laws were supposed to protect everyone, it didn't always work that way. The Mexican citizens of New Mexico were still divided into different classes. As trade increased, the upper classes made far more money than the lower classes. This angered the poor. They felt they were treated unfairly. Some of the poorest people were the **Pueblo** (see p. 36). These were Mexican citizens of Native American descent.

In 1835, the government of Mexico sent Colonel Albino Pérez (*al-BEE-noh per-EZ*) to become governor of New Mexico. He was a high-ranking officer in the Mexican army. Soon after Colonel Pérez arrived, he was ordered by the Mexican government to begin a new type of tax system. The new taxes were much higher. Both the rich and poor were expected to pay these taxes, but the taxes hurt the poor the most.

In 1837, some of the Mexican citizens of New Mexico revolted. The ranchers and Pueblo people joined together to fight. Colonel Pérez left Santa Fe with his army and met the rebel forces at La Mesilla (*lah mess-EE-uh*). The rebel forces defeated Colonel Pérez and his soldiers. Colonel Pérez had done much to make the Pueblo angry.

The rebels enjoyed victory for a short time. They elected their own governor, General Jose Caballero (*ho-SAY cab-AY-air-oh*). Many of the wealthy ranchers had not supported the revolt. They refused to accept General Caballero. A wealthy sheep rancher named **Manuel Armijo** (see p. 101) raised an army against Caballero and defeated him. In 1838, Armijo declared himself the governor of New Mexico. He soon proved to be as harsh a governor as Pérez had been.

Oregon Trail

Route used by settlers traveling west from Missouri to Oregon. In the 1800s, many settlers from the United States. moved westward toward the fertile lands of Oregon, Washington, and **California** (see p. 104). The Oregon Trail was the route many of these settlers chose to take.

A View of the Oregon Trail

Francis Parkman was born in Boston but had great curiosity about the western wilderness and the people who lived there. In 1846, he traveled through the West. Like many other Americans, Parkman knew that the United States was trying to expand its territory. He shared the popular belief in Manifest Destiny. When Parkman completed his travels, he wrote *The Oregon Trail*, a book about his experiences. In this excerpt, Parkman describes a passing wagon train.

We were late in breaking up our camp . . . and scarcely had we ridden a mile when we saw . . . drawn against the horizon, a line of objects stretching . . . along the level edge of the prairie. . . . We saw close before us the . . . caravan, with its heavy white wagons creeping on in slow procession, and a large drove of cattle following behind. Half a dozen . . . Missourians, mounted on horseback, were . . . shouting among them . . . they called out to us: "How are ye, boys? Are ye for Oregon or California?"

As we pushed rapidly by the wagons, children's faces were thrust out from the white coverings to look at us; while the careworn, thin-featured matron . . . seated in front, suspended the knitting on which most of them were engaged to stare at us with wondering curiosity. By the side of each wagon stalked the **proprietor**, urging on his patient oxen . . . inch by inch, on their . . . journey.

◀ **proprietor**
an owner

The Oregon Trail began in Independence, Missouri. It ended about two thousand miles away at Fort Vancouver in what is now the state of Washington. Fur traders and missionaries to the Native Americans had first used the trail. In the 1840s, more than thirteen thousand people traveled from Missouri to the western lands. The journey took from four to six months to complete.

In 1843, a large group of a thousand people traveled together. Like the settlers before them, they started out from Independence, Missouri. Heading northwest to the Platte River, they followed the trail in covered wagons pulled by oxen. They followed the river to Fort Laramie in what is now Wyoming.

There, the settlers got more supplies. Once they were rested, they moved on. The fastest the oxen could travel was about two miles an hour. It was a difficult and dangerous trip. The caravan of wagons, called a *wagon train*, passed through mud and rivers. It struggled through desert and the steep passes of the Rocky Mountains. The travelers suffered from disease, hunger, and bitter cold. Many people died along the way.

Once the wagon train was through the Rocky Mountains, it proceeded to the Snake River. There, the settlers made a choice. They could turn north and continue on the Oregon Trail to Oregon and Washington. They could also leave the trail and turn south toward California. Many settlers chose California.

In 1843, California was still part of the Republic of Mexico. The Mexican government was not pleased to see so many of these settlers arriving in California. Unlike earlier settlers, these settlers had brought their families with them. They considered themselves U.S. citizens. They had no intention of becoming Mexican citizens. The Mexican government began to see the settlers as a threat to the peace of California. As it turned out, the Mexican government was right. The settlers arriving in the 1840s were an important force behind the efforts to make California part of the United States.

Santa Anna, General Antonio López de (1794-1876)

Antonio López de Santa Anna (Library of Congress)

Mexican general and statesman. Antonio López de Santa Anna was born in Jalapa, **Mexico** (see p. 62). His father was a minor official in Mexico while it was under the control of **Spain** (see p. 39). Santa Anna served in the Mexican army throughout his career.

Santa Anna angered many people because he would fight on both sides of an issue. For example, in 1821, he supported Augustín de Iturbide as president of Mexico. In 1823, he changed sides and helped to overthrow Iturbide. In 1828, he helped Vincente Guerrero become Mexico's president. Later, he turned against Guerrero and helped to bring about his downfall. Santa Anna developed a reputation that he could not be trusted. This reputation hurt him many times throughout his life.

In 1829, Santa Anna became a hero to the Mexican people when he helped to win a fight against Spain during the Battle of Tampico. His popularity helped him become elected president of Mexico in 1833. He had made certain promises about how he would govern the people. Once he became president, he broke those promises. In 1836, Santa Anna marched into **Texas** (see p. 91) and defeated the Texan rebels at the **Alamo** (see p. 99). His victory, though, earned him the hatred of the Texans, who then defeated Santa Anna at the Battle of San Jacinto. When Santa Anna returned to Mexico, the Mexican people no longer wanted him as president and he was forced to retire.

In 1836, his fortunes rose when he led an attack against the French who were trying to land at Veracruz. Santa Anna lost a leg during that battle. His actions during the battle won him some regard from the people of Mexico. In 1841, he led a revolt against the president of Mexico. Santa Anna seized power and became a dictator. In 1845, he was forced out of Mexico.

When the U.S.-Mexican War started in 1846, Santa Anna asked President James Polk to send him to Mexico. Santa Anna said he would be able to help bring about peace between the two countries. Instead, he took command of the Mexican troops and led them against the United States. As commander of the Mexican forces, Santa Anna fought against U.S. general Winfield Scott. The Mexicans, led by Santa Anna, fought bravely, but General Scott defeated them. The U.S. forces took Mexico City and forced Santa Anna to leave.

Santa Anna spent most of the rest of his life in exile from Mexico. Two years before his death, he was allowed to return.

Santa Fe Trail

Important trade route from the United States to the Mexican territory of Santa Fe. **Spain** (see p. 39) restricted its territories' trade with other countries during the time it controlled them in North America. This changed when **Mexico** (see p. 62) won its inde-

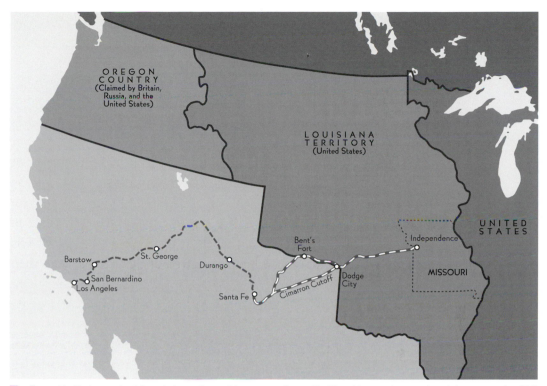

The Santa Fe Trail stretched from Independence, Missouri, to Santa Fe, New Mexico. A second trail, known as the Old Spanish Trail, went from Santa Fe to Los Angeles, California.

pendence from Spain. Mexico welcomed traders from other nations. Santa Fe, in what is now **New Mexico** (see p. 66), was a particularly favorite place for trade. Native Americans traveling west to Santa Fe from what is now Missouri had used this trail since the time before **Christopher Columbus** (see p. 52).

In 1821, an American merchant named William Becknell led a line of mules carrying trade goods from Franklin, Missouri, to Santa Fe. There, he sold everything he had brought. His success started a wave of trade along what became known as the Santa Fe Trail.

Every spring from 1822 until about 1842, trade wagons rolled out of Independence, Missouri, on their way to the markets of Santa Fe. The wagons carried items such as fabric, clothing, tools, kitchen pots and pans, jewelry, buttons, clocks, combs, and writing pens. The wagons even carried wallpaper.

Manufactured goods were hard to find in Santa Fe. This meant that the people lived in simple *adobe* houses. Even the rich did not have much furniture or decoration in their homes. The

"A Foreigner in My Own Land"

Juan Seguín was a Tejano, a Spanish-speaking native of Texas. He had fought with the Texan rebels against Mexico during the Texan Revolution. He eventually became the mayor of San Antonio. In 1842, a Mexican general started spreading a false rumor that Seguín was secretly still loyal to Mexico. Seguín's enemies acted on the rumor. He was forced to leave. In 1858, Seguín wrote about his memories of San Antonio. The book is called *Personal Memoirs of John N. Seguín*. In this excerpt, Seguín tells about the jealousy some Texans had for the wealthy Tejanos. He also describes how he felt being forced to leave the land of his birth.

The jealousy evinced against me by several officers of the companies recently arrived in San Antonio, from the United States, soon spread amongst the American straggling adventurers, who were already beginning to work their dark intrigues against the native families, whose only crime was, that they owned large tracts of land and desirable property. . . . I will also point out the origin of another enmity which on several occasions, endangered my life. In those evil days, San Antonio was swarming with adventurers from every quarter of the globe. Many a noble heart grasped the sword in the defence of the liberty of Texas, cheerfully pouring out their blood for our cause, and to them everlasting public gratitude is due; but there were also many bad men, fugitives from their country, who found in this land an open field for their criminal designs. . . . On my return to San Antonio, several persons told me that the Mexican officers had declared that I was in their favor. This rumor and some threats uttered against me by Goodman, left me but little doubt that my enemies would try to ruin me. . . . Matters being in this state, I saw that it was necessary to take some step which would place me in security, and save my family from constant wretchedness. I had to leave Texas, abandon all for which I had fought and spent my fortune, to become a wanderer. The ingratitude of those, who had assumed to themselves the right of convicting me; their credulity in declaring me a traitor, on mere rumors when I had to plead, in my favor the loyal patriotism with which I had always served Texas, wounded me deeply.

arrival of the trade wagons changed this. The people of Santa Fe and the rest of the New Mexico territory bought whatever they could. They paid for the manufactured goods with gold, silver, beaver furs, animal hides, and wool. The traders would take these items back to the East and sell them.

Sometimes Mexicans living in the New Mexico territory became traders. They traveled the other way, buying manufactured goods in the East and bringing them back to New Mexico and farther south into the Mexican state of Chihuahua (*chi-WAh-WAH*). Most of the time, though, people traveled from the United States into the New Mexico territory.

The Mexican government tried to encourage Americans to come, trade, and then return to the United States. The Mexican government did not want to have too many American settlers. It believed that it had to control the number of American settlers to protect the Mexican way of life. It offered very few land grants to people arriving on the Santa Fe Trail. Traders were welcome. Settlers were not.

Seguín, Juan (1806-1890)

Tejano politician and fighter in the Texan war for independence (see **Texan Revolution**, p. 120). Juan Seguín (*wahn seh-GEEN*) was born into one of the most important Tejano families of **Texas** (see p. 91). The Tejano were Spanish-speaking Mexican citizens who lived in Texas. Seguín's father was one of the first to assist **Stephen Austin** (see p. 102) in bringing colonists from the United States to Texas.

In 1834, Seguín was made the chief administrator of the San Antonio district. Like his father, Juan was a strong supporter of justice and human rights for all Texans. He was alarmed when Mexican president **Antonio López de Santa Anna** (see p. 113) began to ignore some of the rights promised to citizens by the Mexican constitution. Seguín supported Texans in their demands to govern themselves. These sentiments led to Texas's fight for independence from **Mexico** (see p. 62).

When the Texan Revolution began, Seguín stood with the Texan rebels. His decision to help the Texans was difficult. Since he was a Tejano, the Mexican government believed he would be loyal to Mexico. Many Tejanos did remain loyal to Mexico and fought against the Anglo-American Texans in the battles to come. Other Tejanos, like Seguín, fought with the Texans against Mexico.

In 1835, General Martín Cos led a Mexican force into San Antonio. Seguín organized a force of Tejano ranchers. They rode

Juan Seguín (Texas State Library)

to help the Texans at the Siege of Béxar. The Texans succeeded in capturing San Antonio from General Cos. After the victory, Seguín was made a captain in the new Texas army cavalry.

In 1836, **General Santa Anna** (see p. 113) brought Mexican forces into Texas to fight the Texan rebels. His forces surrounded the **mission** (see p. 64) called the **Alamo** (see p. 99). The Texans in the Alamo were terribly outnumbered by the huge Mexican force. Seguín was one of those inside the walls of the Alamo. The commander of the Texan forces in the Alamo chose Seguín to ride to other rebel Texan camps to ask for help. Seguín was chosen because he could speak both Spanish and English. He also knew the area in which he would be traveling. Seguín made it to the camp of the Texan army led by General **Sam Houston** (see p. 107). Houston immediately provided men and supplies to help defend the Alamo. Houston's forces were too late. By the time they arrived, the Alamo had fallen. All the Texan soldiers inside had been killed.

Seguín and his Tejano ranchers then fought alongside **Sam Houston** (see p. 107) at the Battle of San Jacinto. Houston led the rebel Texan forces against Santa Anna and the Mexican army. The Texans defeated Santa Anna's forces. Seguín was promoted to colonel. He was then named commander of the Texas forces in San Antonio.

Once the Republic of **Texas** (see p. 91) was established, Seguín left the army. He was elected to the Texas senate in 1838. After serving in the senate, he became the mayor of San Antonio. Despite his service to the new republic, Seguín and the other Tejanos were very surprised at the treatment they received from some of the Texans they had helped. Many towns in the new Republic of Texas wanted to force out all the Tejanos. Even the people in San Antonio thought about doing this.

In 1842, the Mexican army returned to try to take San

Antonio back from the Republic of Texas. As the mayor of San Antonio, Seguín led the Texan forces against the Mexican army. He succeeded in defeating the Mexicans, but something terrible happened. The Mexican commander started a false rumor that Seguín was secretly still loyal to Mexico. The Texans Seguín had helped accused him of betraying Texas. Seguín was forced to run away to save his life. He went to Mexico.

The Mexican government knew Seguín was not a traitor to Texas. When he arrived in Mexico, they gave him the choice of serving in the Mexican army or going to prison. Seguín chose the army. He was in the army when the **U.S.-Mexican War** (see p. 124) started. During those battles, he had to fight against the people he had once seen as comrades and friends.

Despite the poor treatment he had received, Seguín wanted to return to Texas. He had been born there. He considered Texas his home. Seguín received permission from the U.S. government to return. When he returned, though, the Texans continued to torment him. They made his life very hard. In 1867, Seguín went back to Mexico. He died there in 1890.

In later years, Seguín's service to Texas was finally recognized. He is considered a hero to many Hispanic Americans. The city of Seguín is named in his honor. On October 28, 2000, a large statue of Seguín mounted on a horse was unveiled in the city that bears his name.

Spanish Trail

Trade route from Santa Fe to **California** (see p. 104). In 1776, two Spanish priests created a trail that led from Santa Fe to Los Angeles, California. Father Silvestre Vélez (*sil-VES-tray vel-EZ*) and Father José Juan Dominguez (*ho-SAY wahn doh-MIN-gehz*) planned to use the trail to travel more easily among the Spanish **missions** (see p. 64) throughout the area.

In 1829, a Santa Fe merchant named Antonio Armijo led an *expedition* of sixty people along the old trail that the priests had blazed. They camped at a site about a hundred miles from what is now the city of Las Vegas, Nevada. Scouts from this group found a good source of water. The water allowed Armijo to create a shorter trail than the one the priests had made. This new trail allowed traders to cut through the desert. This was better than having to go around the desert as they had to do in the past. Spanish traders called the place where the water was found "Las Vegas," which means "the Meadows."

In 1830, Armijo led the first train of pack mules carrying trade goods on the new Spanish Trail from Santa Fe, New Mexico, to Los Angeles, California. The Spanish Trail became a well-used trade route between the two cities.

Texan Revolution (1835-1836)

Events leading to **Texas** (see p. 91) winning independence from **Mexico** (see p. 63). By the 1830s, there were many more Texans of Anglo-American descent living in Texas than there were Mexican American Tejanos, Anglo-American Texans, or just "Texans," who were English-speaking settlers who had crossed the border from the United States into the Mexican territory of Texas. The Tejanos were the Spanish-speaking Mexican citizens of Texas. As more and more settlers arrived, serious disagreements began to spring up between the two groups.

Many Tejanos were offended by some of the customs of the Anglo-American Texans. Mexico had wanted the settlers from the United States to be Roman Catholics. Instead, most of the settlers were Protestants. Mexico did not allow slavery. Many of the Anglo-American settlers came from the South and owned enslaved Americans. The Mexican government had invited the settlers from the United States to come into its country. It had helped them get lands. Many of the Tejanos expected the Texans to become good Mexican citizens like themselves.

The Texans did not see the situation the same way. The Texans felt they had every right to do as they pleased. They began to feel that all of Texas belonged to them. They were not willing to accept the rules laid down by the Mexican government.

The Mexican government became concerned that it would lose Texas. It began to pass laws to prevent more Anglo-American settlers from coming to Texas. One law said that no more slaves could come into Texas. Another law said that no more settlers could enter from the United States. The Mexican government raised taxes on goods coming into Texas from the United States. This made it harder for the settlers to buy the things they needed.

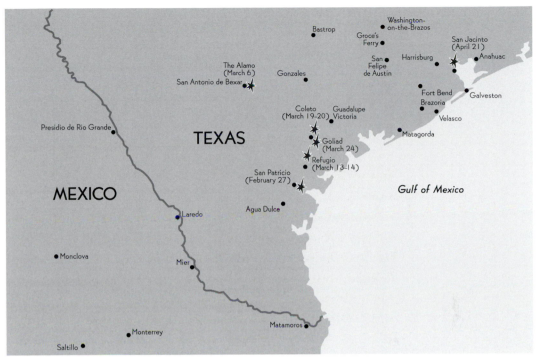

Major battles of the Texan Revolution.

The Texans' anger at the Mexican government grew.

In 1833, **Stephen Austin** (see p. 102) went to Mexico City as a representative of the Texans. He asked the Mexican government to change the laws it had just passed. He also wanted Mexico to make Texas a Mexican state but with a separate constitution based on the U.S. Constitution. At the same time that Austin was making his request, the Mexicans were experiencing problems in their own government. The Mexicans were busy and did not respond to Austin's requests.

After eleven weeks, Austin sent a letter to the city council in San Antonio. He suggested that Texas should form its own state government even though the Mexican government had not given its approval. The Mexican government heard of the Texans' plans. They placed Stephen Austin in prison. Angered, the Texans rebelled against Mexico. They declared their independence on November 7, 1835. This was intended to be a temporary independence. The Texan rebels still hoped they would be granted permission to be a special type of state within the Mexican Republic. This was not to be.

The Texan rebels had already begun their military battles

with the Mexican government in October 1835 at a town called Gonzales (*gahn-ZOLL-ez*). The rebels had refused to return a cannon to the Mexicans. They drove off the Mexican forces with rifle fire. Next, the rebels captured the presidio at Goliad. The rebels then moved on to San Antonio. They laid siege to the city. This means the rebels prevented anyone from entering or leaving the city. On December 11, 1835, the rebels captured San Antonio. They released the commander of the Mexican forces in San Antonio along with his soldiers. His name was General Martín Cos. He was the brother-in-law of General Santa Anna.

General Santa Anna's desire for revenge over the defeat at San Antonio led to the best-known battle of the Texan Revolution. This was the Battle of the **Alamo** (see p. 99). On February 26, 1836, General Santa Anna began his attack on the **mission** (see p. 64) called the Alamo. It ended thirteen days later with the defeat of the rebels' forces. The Battle of the Alamo became the sorrowful memory that made the Texan rebels fight even harder. While Santa Anna was at the Alamo, the Texan government had declared independence from Mexico for good. It gave up all ideas of becoming part of the Mexican Republic. The Texans now wanted to be totally independent of Mexico.

The Battle of San Jacinto on April 21, 1836, was the turning point for the Texan Revolution. General **Sam Houston** (see p. 107) led the Texan rebel army. The rebels defeated General Santa Anna's Mexican forces in a bloody battle. The Texan rebels took terrible revenge for General Santa Anna's actions at the Alamo.

After the Battle of San Jacinto, General Santa Anna moved his army south of the Rio Grande. The Texans formed the Republic of Texas. The republic became known as the **Lone Star Republic** (see p. 109).

Treaty of Guadalupe Hidalgo (1848)

Important treaty signed after the war between the United States and Mexico. In 1848, after two years of war, Mexico signed the Treaty of Guadalupe Hidalgo (*gwah-del-OOP hee-DAHL-goh*). As part of this treaty, or agreement, Mexico surrendered about half of its North American territory to the United States. This territory was all the land north of the Rio Grande and Gila Rivers. The region included present-day **California** (see p. 104), Nevada,

Utah, **New Mexico** (see p. 66), Texas, and parts of Colorado and Wyoming. The United States agreed to pay Mexico $15 million for this land. American settlers had made claims against the Mexican government during the time that **Mexico** (see p. 62) controlled this land. As part of the treaty, the United States agreed to pay these claims.

The Mexican people who settled in these areas were given one year to decide whether they wanted to become U.S. citizens. If they chose not to, they would have to move south to Mexico. If they chose to become U.S. citizens, the U.S. government promised to protect the Mexican residents' property rights. The United States also promised to protect the Mexicans' right to freely practice their religion.

The area of land the United States gained through the Treaty

The United States gained control of California, Nevada, Utah, New Mexico, and parts of Arizona, Colorado, and Wyoming after the U.S.-Mexican War.

of Guadalupe Hidalgo was even larger than the land gained through the Louisiana Purchase in 1803.

U.S.-Mexican War (1846-1848)

U.S. war with **Mexico** (see p. 63) over disagreements concerning the boundary between Texas and Mexico. Trouble between Mexico and the U.S. government had been building for many years. The Mexicans were suspicious of all the U.S. settlers arriving in Mexican-held territory. Settlers poured into **California** (see p. 104) and **New Mexico** (see p. 66). As these settlers arrived, they demanded more and more freedom from Mexico. Mexico knew that the United States wanted to expand as far as it could go. The United States had tried many times between the years of 1821 and 1846 to buy lands that Mexico controlled. Texas was a particular point of disagreement between Mexico and the United States.

Mexico had never accepted the loss of Texas after the Texans declared independence in 1835. The Mexicans and Texans also strongly disagreed about the border between them. Mexico claimed that Mexican territory ran all the way to the Nueces River. The Texans said the border was the Rio Grande. As far as Mexico was concerned, the territory between the Nueces River and the Rio Grande belonged to Mexico. The border problem continued to worsen between 1835 and 1845.

In 1845, President James Polk sent a diplomat named John Slidell to Mexico to try one more time to buy territory from Mexico. He hoped Mexico would agree to give to the United States a large part of Mexican territory reaching from Texas to the Pacific Ocean. This area included the present-day states of New Mexico, Arizona, Nevada, Utah, and California.

Slidell also intended to persuade the Mexican government to agree to the Rio Grande as the border between Texas and Mexico. The Mexicans refused to see him. They would not agree to any of his requests.

While Slidell was in Mexico, Texas became part of the United States. This action so infuriated the Mexicans that they broke off all government communication with the United States. On January 13, 1846, President Polk ordered U.S. troops under General Zachary Taylor to the Texas side of the Rio Grande.

The Battle of Buena Vista

Sergeant Benjamin Franklin Scribner was a young soldier with the Indiana Volunteers. He was part of the U.S. Army under General Zachary Taylor. The troops fought at Buena Vista during the U.S.-Mexican War. In this excerpt, Scribner describes the beginning of the battle when the U.S. forces faced the much larger Mexican army. He also describes his feelings upon seeing one of his fellow soldiers shot during the battle.

Heavy fire was kept up till dark, when all was silent, save the echoing of the enemy's trumpets. I never shall forget the peculiar melody of those sounds as we lay upon our arms, hungry, and shivering with cold. It was a prelude to the awful **din** of the next day. . . . At sunrise, on the following day, the roaring of the enemy's cannon announced the commencement of hostilities. A heavy fire was opened upon our riflemen upon the mountain, but they returned it in a handsome style. . . . The whole mountain side, as far as they eye could reach, glittered with the enemy's bayonets and lances. . . . We formed a line in front of three regiments of Mexico's oldest soldiers. It was an awful moment to face the thousands of veterans in solid columns, with their **gaudy** uniforms and showy banners. But we had no time for admiration; for, before our line was formed, they had fired two rounds, which we soon returned in right good earnest. . . . About this time, the battery on our left galled us exceedingly. It appeared as if we had purposely halted in their exact range, and the whole atmosphere resounded with the whizzing shot that came with increasing precision. Apollos Stephens was the first of the Greys to fall. He received a grape shot in the head, and fell back almost into my arms. O, how shall I describe the horror of my feelings? There lay quivering in death one of my comrades, with his eyes upturned, and the tears starting from them. It was a sad and touching scene—one that will never be effaced from my memory.

◀ **din**
noise

◀ **gaudy**
fancy looking but
without substance

President Polk knew that the Mexican government would see this as an invasion of Mexican territory. He knew it was likely that the Mexicans would start a fight. On April 25, Mexican forces crossed the Rio Grande and started a battle with a small section

The U.S.-Mexican War was fought on two fronts. The main one was south of the Río Grande, in what is still Mexican territory today. The battles took place in California, both in the south and in the San Francisco area. With Mexico's defeat in the war, California, and much of the rest of Mexico's Far North, became U.S. territory.

of the U.S. Army. General Taylor sent word to President Polk that the battle had taken place. This was what President Polk needed. He asked Congress to declare war on Mexico. Congress agreed, and on May 13, 1846, the U.S.-Mexican War began.

Between 1846 and 1848, U.S. forces invaded Mexico, New Mexico, and California. General Zachary Taylor and General Winfield Scott focused on northern Mexico. A separate U.S. army, called the "Army of the West," conquered New Mexico and California. The Mexicans fought hard. For two years, they tried to stop the U.S. Army from pushing farther and farther into Mexican territory. Most of the time, the U.S. forces had better-trained soldiers and better weapons. The Mexican army usually had more soldiers.

In Mexico, the fighting was the harshest. The Mexican army did everything it could to protect its capital of Mexico City. In

February 1847, Zachary Taylor captured Buena Vista. This was the first U.S. victory. In March, General Scott landed a large force at Veracruz. He captured the fort there and started to move toward Mexico City. The U.S. forces captured town after town. The Mexican army did not give up easily. As the U.S. Army drew closer to Mexico City, the fighting intensified. The battles of Molino del Rey and Chapultupec were particularly vicious because they were the last defenses of Mexico City. General Scott's army defeated the Mexican forces in both battles. By September 1847, the U.S. forces were in Mexico City. The U.S.-Mexican War ended with the **Treaty of Guadalupe Hidalgo** (see p. 122) on February 2, 1848.

Vallejo, Mariano Guadalupe (1808–1890)

Mexican commander and **California** (see p. 104) legislator. Mariano Guadalupe Vallejo was born in an upper-class California Mexican family. California Mexicans were also called *Californios*.

Mariano Vallejo (Library of Congress)

Vallejo became a cadet in the Mexican army at age fifteen. When he was twenty-one, he led a successful *expedition* against a Native American revolt in San José. He continued to do well in the Mexican army. In time, he became the military commander of northern California.

Even though he held an important position of responsibility, Vallejo was very critical of the Mexican government. All his life he had sympathized with the group of people known as Mexican liberals. This group stressed the importance of government ruled by law. They felt that the powers of government should be defined by a constitution. They also believed that there should be a separation between the powers of the state and religion. Many of the beliefs of the Mexican liberals were the same as those put forth by the ideals of the U.S. government. The liberals saw the U.S. government as an example of a good government.

In 1836, Vallejo supported a rebellion in northern California that led to California being named a "free state." Vallejo's nephew, Juan Baptista Alvarado (*whan bap-TEES-tuh al-vuh-RAHD-oh*), led this rebellion. The Mexican government quickly put down the rebellion. Despite Vallejo's support of the rebellion, he was allowed to keep his post as military commander.

Vallejo was a very wealthy landowner. Unlike many wealthy Mexican landowners, however, he welcomed Anglo-American settlers to California. He helped them find land to settle. Even though he was a Mexican citizen, Vallejo supported the new settlers' efforts to make California independent of Mexico.

In 1846, American rebels led by General John Frémont mounted a revolt to free California from Mexico's rule. Considering his support of the rebels' goals, Vallejo was very surprised at how badly he was treated by them. He and his brother were placed under arrest at Sutter's Fort. They were kept unjustly imprisoned for several months during the fighting against Mexico. When he was released finally, he returned to his estates to find them badly damaged. Many of his possessions had been stolen during the fighting.

Once the United States formally took possession of California, things improved for Vallejo. He became one of eight Californios to serve as a delegate to a state constitutional convention. Vallejo was also elected to the first California state senate.

Vallejo was one of the leading members of California's Mexican community. However, he often saw himself and his fellow Californios treated as foreigners by the new settlers arriving in California. The **Treaty of Guadalupe Hidalgo** (see p. 122) was supposed to protect the property of Vallejo and native Mexicans like him, but it did not. Vallejo eventually lost almost all of his estates. The number of Anglo-Americans continued to rise. Soon, there were many more Anglo-Americans than Californios living in California.

Glossary

adobe: the sun-dried brick made of clay used by Pueblo peoples of the Southwest for building.

alpaca: a South American animal, similar to a llama, that is known for its fleecy wool.

astronomy: the scientific study of the universe beyond the earth.

buffer: something that comes between two rival powers, lessening the chance of a conflict.

constitution: a nation or state's set of laws. Most nations with constitutions have them in written form, such as the United States Constitution.

conversos: a Spanish or Portuguese Jew who converted outwardly to Christianity in the late Middle Ages so as to avoid persecution or expulsion, though often continuing to practice Judaism in secret.

converting: persuading or forcing someone to adopt a particular religion, faith, or belief.

Creoles: people of mixed African and European ancestry who speak a mixed language, especially one based on Spanish or French.

cultural: relating to culture, or all of the ways of behavior, arts, beliefs, institutions, and ways of living of a particular group or community of people.

doctrine: a statement of official policy, especially in foreign affairs and military strategy. Also, a group of principles or beliefs held by a particular religious, political, or scientific group.

expedition: a journey taken by a group of people with a definite purpose in mind, such as discovery or military conquest.

guerrilla: a member of a military or unit operating in small bands in occupied territory. Guerrilla forces often use sudden surprise attacks against their enemies, attacking quickly and then disappearing only to attack again later.

irrigation: the system of watering by means of ditches or artificial channels or by sprinklers.

isthmus: a narrow strip of land connecting two larger masses of land.

keeled: a keeled boat is one that has a keel for the main structure, or backbone, of the boat. The keel, which contains a long ridge that helps guide the boat forward in the water, extends from the front, or bow, of the boat to the stern, or back.

maize: a Spanish translation for the Taino people's word *mahiz*, meaning corn.

militia: a nonprofessional citizen's army, as opposed to the regular professional army.

missionary: a person sent to do religious or charitable work in a foreign country.

monk: a member of a religious brotherhood living in a monastery and devoted to a way of life set by the religious order. The two orders of Catholic monks at work in New Spain were the Jesuits and Franciscans.

New World: the term given to North and South America by European explorers and settlers. Although the Americas were not in fact new, they were new to the Europeans. They called Europe and Asia the Old World.

nomads: members of a nation or tribe with no permanent home, who move from place to place hunting and gathering food.

obsidian: a kind of volcanic glass that is usually black or contains bands. Obsidian is shiny when broken, and was often used for making spearpoints, knives, and other weapons.

pagan: someone with no religion; sometimes the word was specifically used to mean someone who was not a Christian.

plantation: a large estate or farm on which crops are raised, often by workers who live on the plantation. Until the late nineteenth century, many of those workers on plantations throughout North and South America were enslaved Native Americans or Africans.

privateers: a ship privately owned and crewed but authorized by a government during wartime to attack and capture enemy vessels. English privateers frequently attacked Spanish treasure ships.

quinoa: a plant that is native to the Andes Mountains of South America and is cultivated for its edible seeds.

vandalism: the act of destroying public or private property.

war dogs: dogs used in war. Some Spanish conquistadors used war dogs to attack and kill victims.

Resources

General Subjects

BOOKS

Gernand, Renèe. *The Cuban Americans*. New York: Chelsea House Publishers, 1996.

Hoyt-Goldsmith, Diane. *Celebrating a Quinceañera: A Latina's fifteenth birthday celebration*. New York: Holiday House, 2002.

_____. *Las Posadas: An Hispanic Christmas celebration*. New York: Holiday House, 1999.

Kanellos, Nicolás, ed. *The Hispanic American Almanac: A Reference Work on Hispanics in the United States*. Detroit: Gale Research, 1977.

_____. *Hispanic Firsts: 500 Years of Extraordinary Achievement*. Detroit: Gale Research, 1997.

Kanellos, Nicolás, with Cristelia Pérez. *Chronology of Hispanic American History*. Detroit: Gale Research, 1997.

Lankford, Mary D. *Quinceanera: A Latina's Journey to Womanhood*. Brookfield, CT: Millbrook Press, 1994.

Martinez, Elizabeth. *500 Years of Chicano History in Pictures*. Expanded and updated ed. Albuquerque: SouthWest Organizing Project, 1991.

Morey, Janet. *Famous Mexican Americans*. New York: Cobblehill Books, 1989.

Ochoa, George. *Atlas of Hispanic American History*. New York: Facts on File, 2002.

Ochoa, George and the New York Public Library. *The New York Public Library Amazing Hispanic American History: A Book of Answers for Kids*. New York: John Wiley and Sons, 1998.

Sinnott, Susan. *Extraordinary Hispanic Americans*. Chicago: Children's Press, 1991.

Smith, Carter and David Lindroth. *Hispanic-American Experience on File*. New York: Facts on File, 1999.

Wohl, Gary and Carmen Cadilla Ruibal. *Hispanic Personalities: Celebrities of the Spanish-Speaking World*. New York: Regents Publishing Company, 1978.

WEBSITES

AfroCuba Web: http://www.afrocubaweb.com/

The Azteca Web page: http://www.azteca.net/aztec/index.shtml

Celebrate Hispanic Heritage!: http://teacher.scholastic.com/activities/hispanic/index.htm

Celebrating Hispanic Heritage: http://www.galegroup.com/free_resources/chh/

El Museo del Barrio: http://www.elmuseo.org/

Famous Hispanics in the World and History: http://coloquio.com/famosos/

Hispanic America U.S.A.: http://www.neta.com/~1stbooks/index.html

History Channel–Hispanic Heritage Month:
http://www.historychannel.com/classroom/hhm/HHM_home_c.html

Homeschool Learning Network–Celebrate Hispanic Heritage!:
http://www.homeschoollearning.com/units/unit_09-13-01.shtml

History and Biography
(Before 1848)

BOOKS

Kirkwood, Burton. *The History of Mexico*. Westport, CT: Greenwood Press, 1998.

Ochoa, George. *The Fall of Mexico City*. Englewood Cliffs: Silver Burdett Press, 1989.

———. *Students Almanac of Native American History*, Vol 1. Westport, CT: Greenwood Press, 2003.

Stanton, Edward F. *Culture and Customs of Spain*. Westport, CT: Greenwood Press, 2002.

VIDEO
Spanish Empire. A National Park Service Film; Harpers Ferry Historical Association.

WEBSITES

AncientMexico.com: The art, history and ancient culture of Mesoamerica:
http://www.ancientmexico.com/

The California Missions Site: http://www.californiamissions.com/

Colonization and Settlement (1542-1774):
http://www.neta.com/%7E1stbooks/defen1a.htm

Hispanic Exploration & Conquest of North America (1492–1541):
http://www.neta.com/%7E1stbooks/defen1.htm

Hispanic History in the Americas:
http://teacher.scholastic.com/activities/hispanic/americas.htm

Hispanics in the American Revolution: http://www.neta.com/%7E1stbooks/revolt_0.htm

San Antonio Missions National Historic Park:
http://www.nps.gov/saan/

Texas, Texans, and the Alamo:
http://www.cah.utexas.edu/exhibits/TexasExhibit/Texas1.html

Web de Anza: http://anza.uoregon.edu/

History and Biography

(Since 1876)

BOOKS

Cedeno, Maria E. *Cesar Chavez: Labor Leader.* Brookfield, CT: Millbrook Press, 1993.

Collins, David R. *Farmworker's Friend: The Story of Cesar Chavez.* Minneapolis: Carolrhoda Books, 1996.

Conord, Bruce W. *Cesar Chavez.* New York: Chelsea Juniors, 1992.

Faistein, Mark. *Cesar Chavez.* Paramus, NJ: Globe Fearon, 1994.

VIDEO

Agueda Martinez–Our People, Our Country. Moctesuma Esparza Productions, Inc. Educational Media Corporation, 1977.

Chicano. J. Gary Mitchell; BFA Educational Media, 1971.

Decision at Delano. California Newsreel; MGM/UA Home Video, 1967.

El Teatro Campesino. National Educational Television, Indiana University AV Center, 1970.

Harvest of Shame. CBS News; CRM/McGraw Hill Films, 1960.

WEBSITES

Hispanics in the American Civil War: http://www.neta.com/%7E1stbooks/revolt_0.htm

The Spanish American War in Motion Pictures:
http://memory.loc.gov/ammem/sawhtml/sawhome.html

Zoot Suit Riots: http://www.pbs.org/wgbh/amex/zoot/eng_tguide/index.html

VIDEO

Viva La Causa! 500 Years of Chicano History. Southwest Organizing Project and Collision Course Video Productions. San Francisco, CA: Collision Course Video Productions, 1995.

Yo Soy Chicano. KCET, Los Angeles; PBS, Public Broadcasting System; New York: Cinema Guild.

Folklore, Fiction and Poetry

BOOKS

Alarcón, Francisco X. *From the Bellybutton of the Moon and Other Summer Poems/Del Ombligo de la Luna y Otro Poemas de Verano.* New York: Children's Book Press, 1998.

Alicea, Gil C., with Carmine DeSena. *The Air Down Here: True Tales from a South Bronx Boyhood.* San Francisco: Chronicle Books, 1995.

Alvarez, Julia. *Before We Were Free.* New York: Knopf, 2003.

Argueta, Jorge. *A Movie in My Pillow.* New York: Children's Book Press, 2002.

Cumpian, Carlos. *Latino Rainbow: Poems about Latino Americans.* Chicago: Children's Press, 1994.

Herrera, Juan Felipe. *Crashboomlove.* Albuquerque: University of New Mexico Press, 1999.

Joseph, Lynn. *The Color of My Words.* New York: HarperCollins, 2000.

Martinez, Victor. *Parrot in the Oven: Mi Vida.* New York: Joanna Cotler/HarperCollins, 1996.

Bibliography

Acuña, Rudolfo. *Occupied America: The Chicano's Struggle Toward Liberation*. New York: Harper and Row, 1972.

Altamira, Rafael. *A History of Spain: From the Beginnings to the Present Day*. New York: D. Van Nostrand Co., 1948.

Bazant, Jan. *A Concise History of Mexico*. New York: Cambridge University Press, 1985.

Berger, Josef. *Discovers of the New World*. Mahwah, NJ: Troll Associates, 1960.

Boswell, Thomas, and James Curtis. *The Cuban-American Experience: Culture, Images and Perspectives*. Totowa, NJ: Rowan and Allanheld, 1983.

Calavita, Kitty. *Inside the State: The Bracero Program, Immigration and the I.N.S.* New York: Routledge, 1992.

Chapman, Victoria, and David Lindroth. *Latin American History on File*. New York: Facts on File, 1996.

Crow, John A. *The Epic of Latin America*. Berkeley: University of California Press, 1971.

Dor-Ner, Zvi, and William Sheller. *Columbus and the Age of Discovery*. New York: Morrow, 1991.

Ehrlich, Paul, et al. *The Golden Door: International Migration, Mexico, and the United States*. New York: Ballantine Books, 1979.

Fernández-Shaw, Carlos. *The Hispanic Presence in North America from 1492 to Today*. New York: Facts On File, 1987.

García, Juan Ramon. *Operation Wetback*. Westport, CT: Greenwood Press, 1980.

Grann, L.H., and Peter J. Duignan. *The Hispanics in the United States*. Boulder, CO, and London: Westview Press, 1986.

Guerin-Gonzalez, Camille. *Mexican Workers and American Dreams: Immigrants, Repatriation, and California Farm Labor: 1900–1939*. New Brunswick, NJ: Rutgers University Press, 1994.

Hardin, Stephen, and Gary S. Zaboly. *Texian Iliad: A Military History of the Texas Revolution.* Austin: University of Texas Press, 1994.

Jiménez, Carlos M. *The Mexican American Heritage.* Berkeley, CA: TQS Publications, 1994.

Kanellos, Nicolás, ed. *The Hispanic American Almanac.* Detroit: Gale Research, 1993.

Krell, Dorothy, ed. *The California Missions: A Pictorial History.* Menlo Park, CA: Sunset Publishing Corporation, 1991.

Lewin, Stephen, ed. *The Latino Experience in U.S. History.* Paramus, NJ: Globe Fearon Educational Publisher, 1994.

Library of Congress. "Hispanic Americans in Congress, 1822–1995." Available online. URL: http://lcweb.loc.gov/rr/hispanic/congress/munozrivera.html. Downloaded June 12, 1999.

Mazón, Mauricio. *The Zoot-Suit Riots.* Austin: University of Texas Press, 1984.

Meier, Matt, and Feliciano Rivera. *Dictionary of Mexican American History.* Westport, CT: Greenwood Press, 1981.

Nevin, David. *The Mexican War.* Alexandria, VA: Time-Life Books, 1978.

Novas, Himilce. *Everything You Need to Know About Latino History.* New York: Dutton, 1994.

Pitt, Leonard. *The Decline of the Californios: A Social History of the Spanish-Speaking Californians, 1846–1890.* Berkeley: University of California Press, 1970.

Reddy, Marlita. *Statistical Record of Hispanic Americans.* Detroit: Gale Research, 1993.

Samora, Julian, and Patricia Vandel Simon. *A History of the Mexican-American People.* Notre Dame, IN: University of Notre Dame Press, 1977.

Sanchez, George. *Becoming Mexican-American: Ethnicity, Culture, and Identity in Chicano Los Angeles 1900–1945.* New York: Oxford University Press, 1993.

Smith, Carter, ed. *The Explorers and Settlers.* Brookfield, CT: Millbrook Press, 1991.

Smith, Joseph. *The Spanish-American War: Conflict in the Caribbean and the Pacific, 1895–1902.* New York: Longman, 1994.

Thernstrom, Stephan, ed. *Harvard Encyclopedia of American Ethnic Groups.* Cambridge, MA: The Belknap Press, 1980.

Index

Note: The index below contains entries for both volumes of the Student Almanac *of Hispanic American History. The roman numeral I refers to pages in the first volume. The roman numeral II refers to pages in the second volume.*